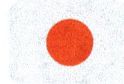

SOUL OF JAPAN
Photography Journal

Lucia Bustamante

It was love at first sight.
The breeze, the silence, the taste, the beauty.

THE URBAN

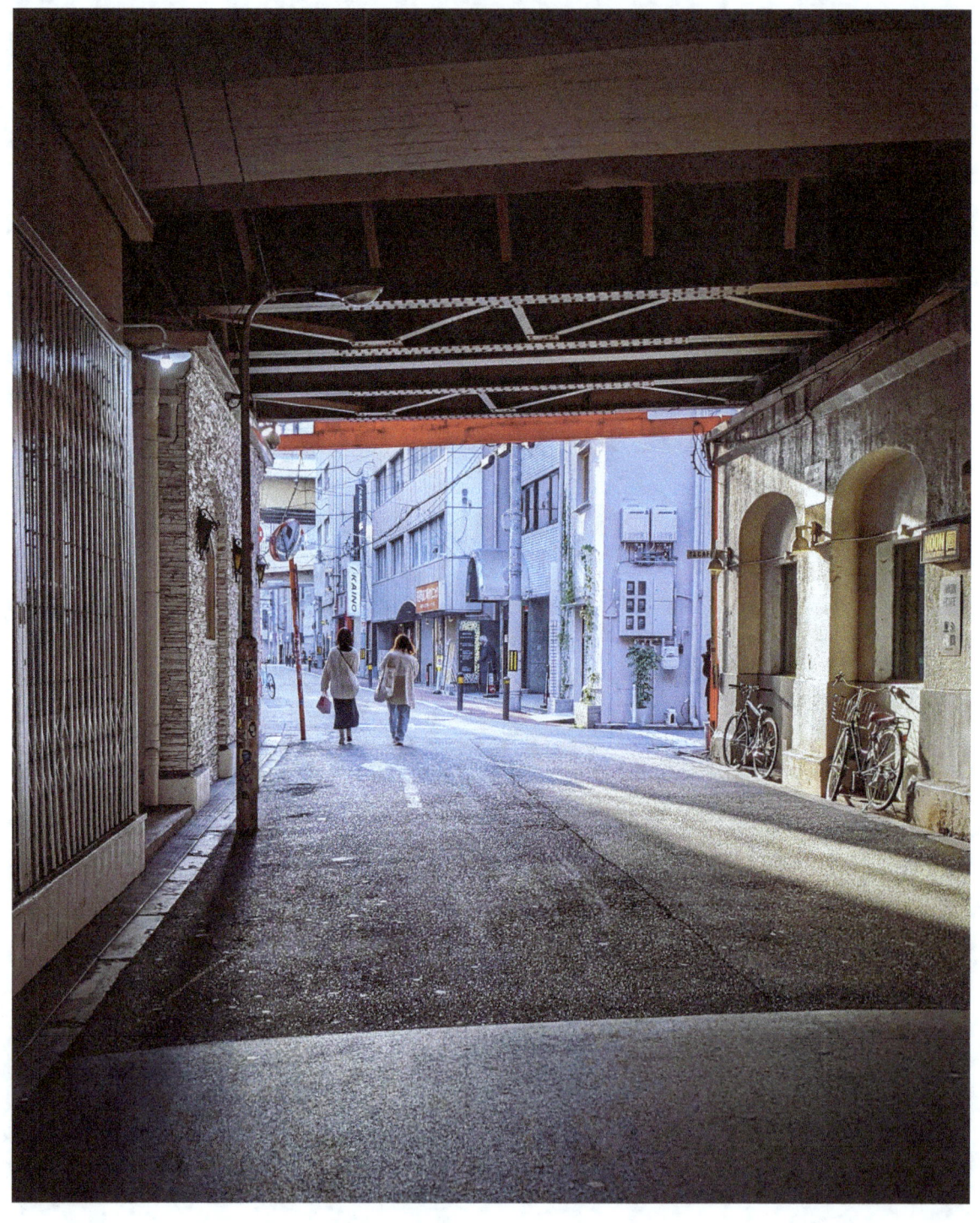

Every corner of Tokyo is a beautiful frame, the city is a stage for endless photographs.

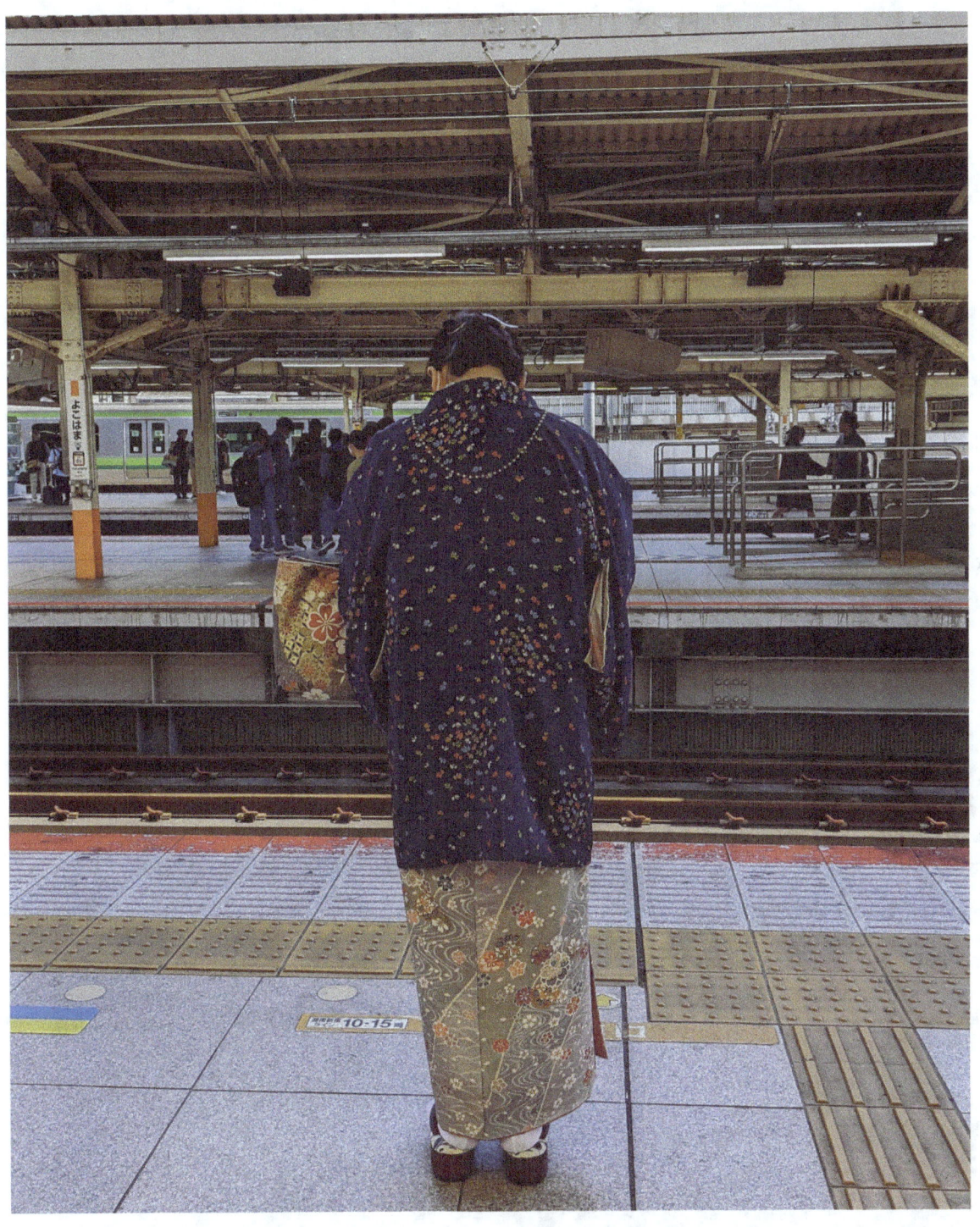

The scenery of the subway, faces, clothes,
people, stories...

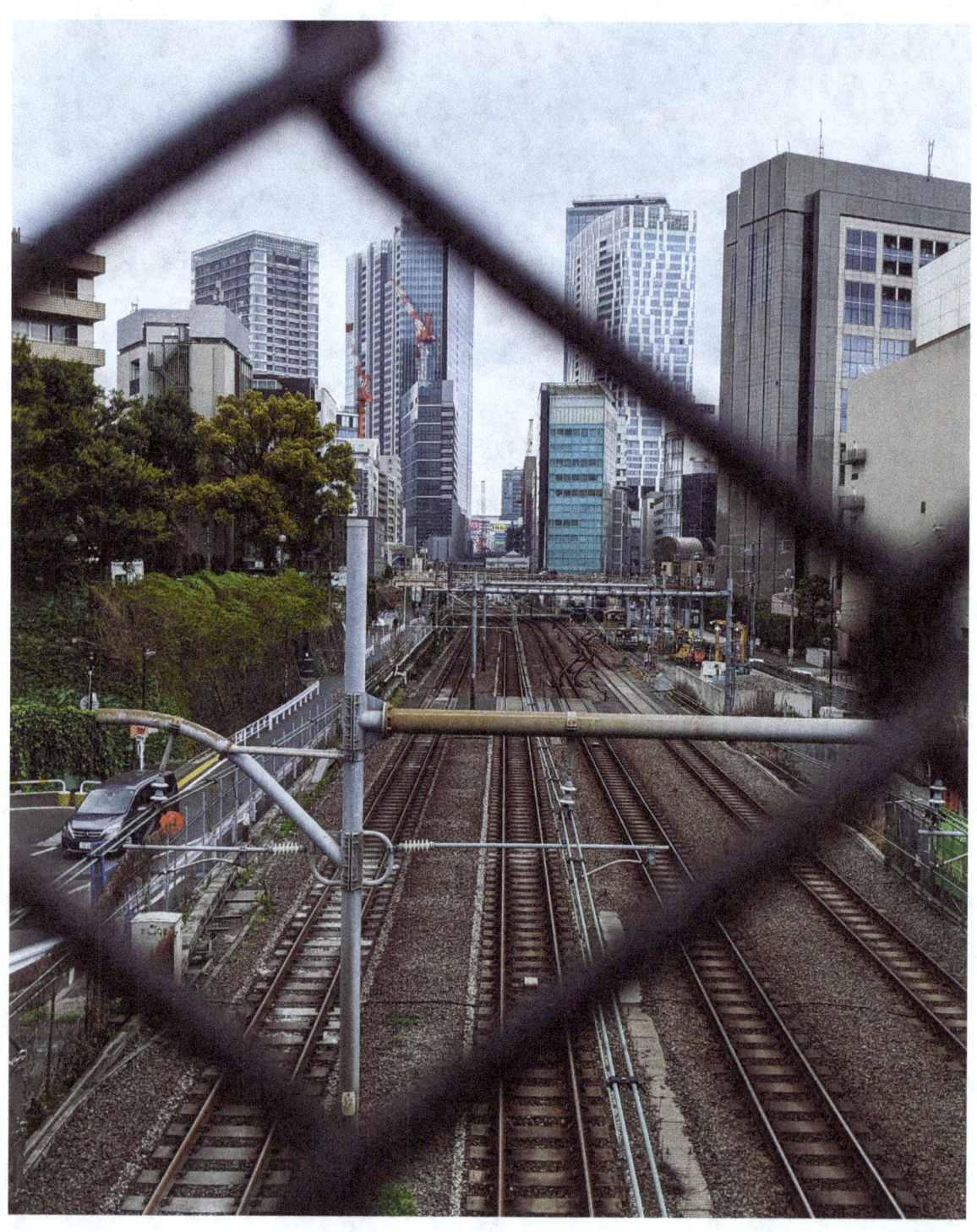

Shibuya 9:46 am.

The dark beauty of the mournful cry of crows.

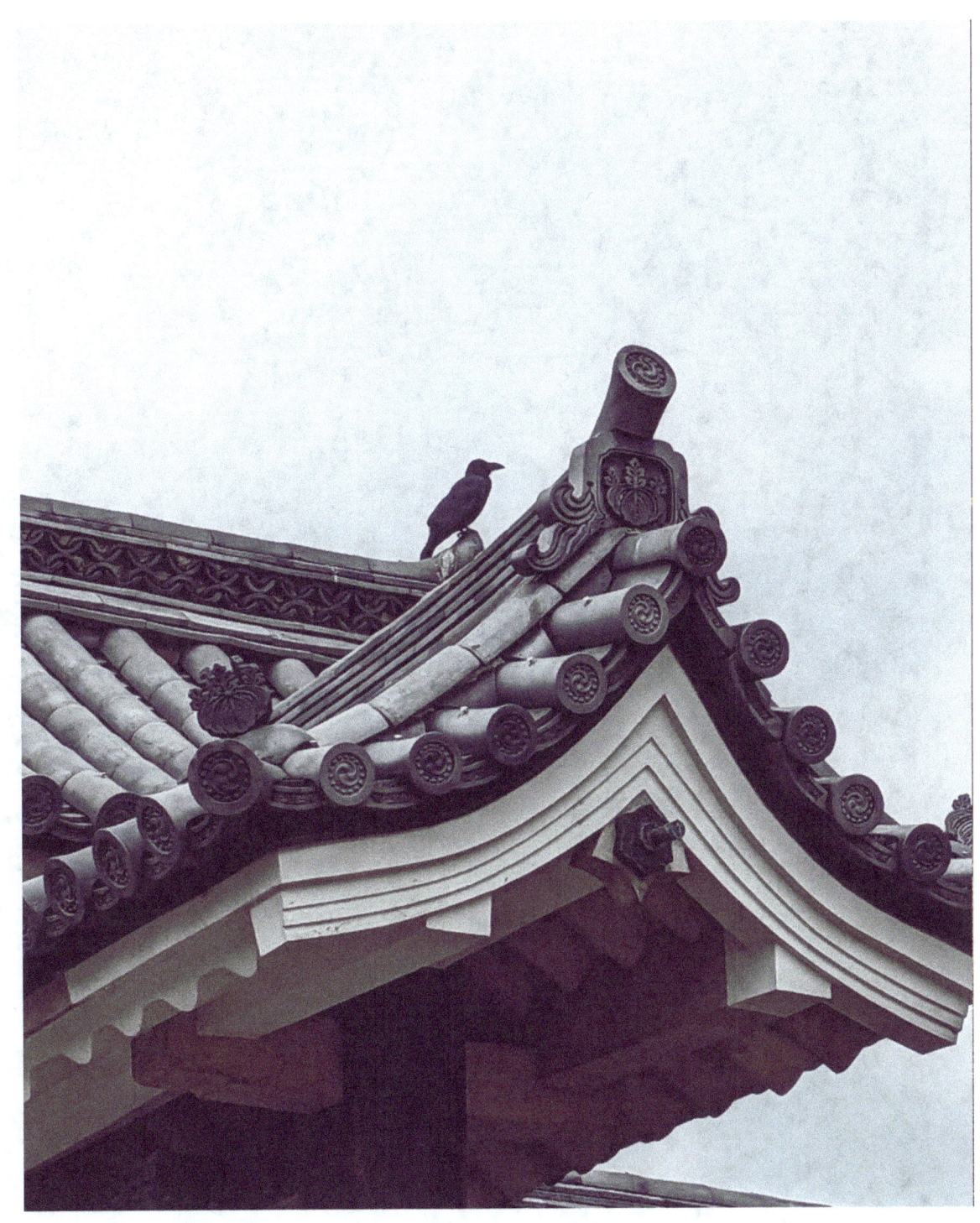

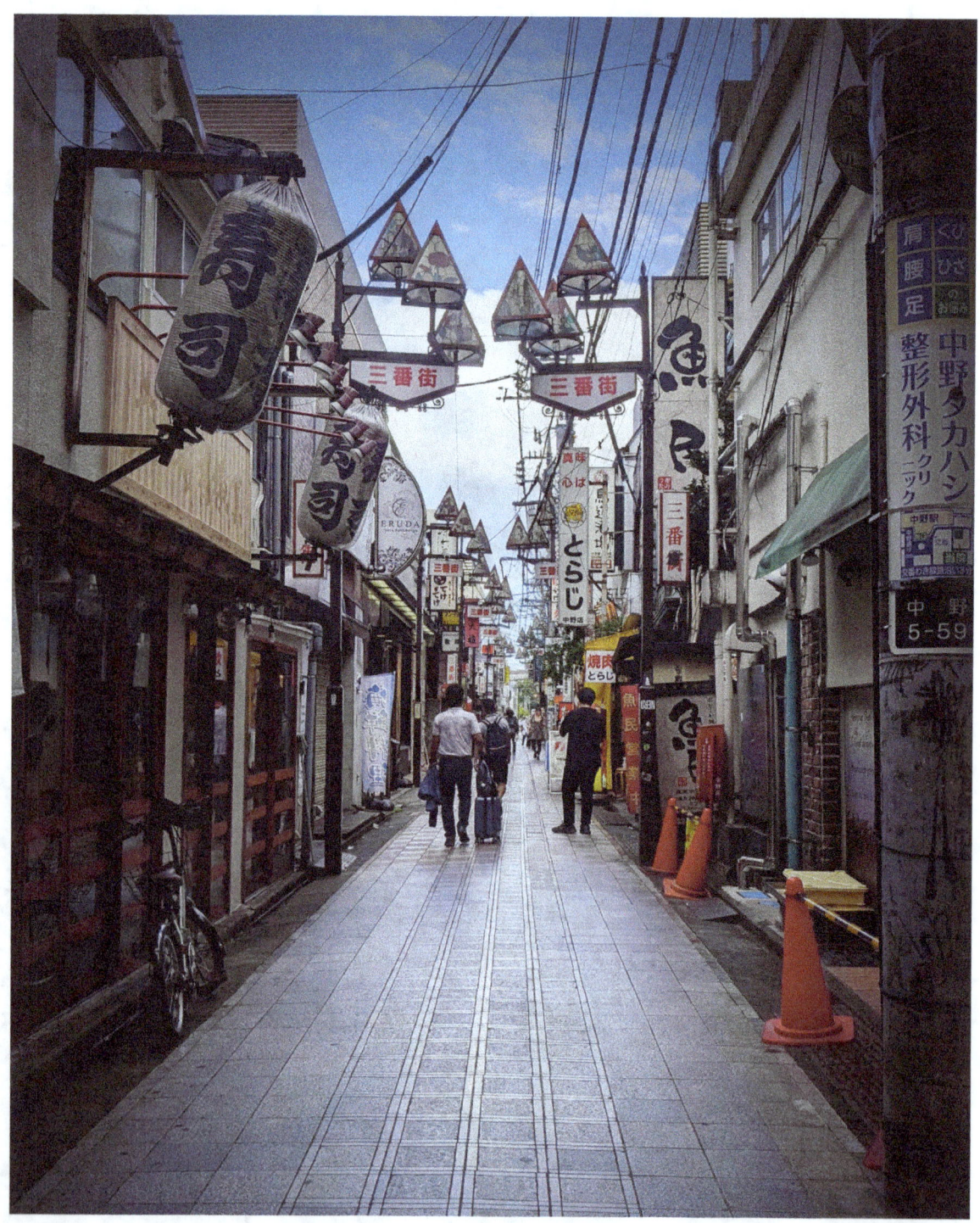

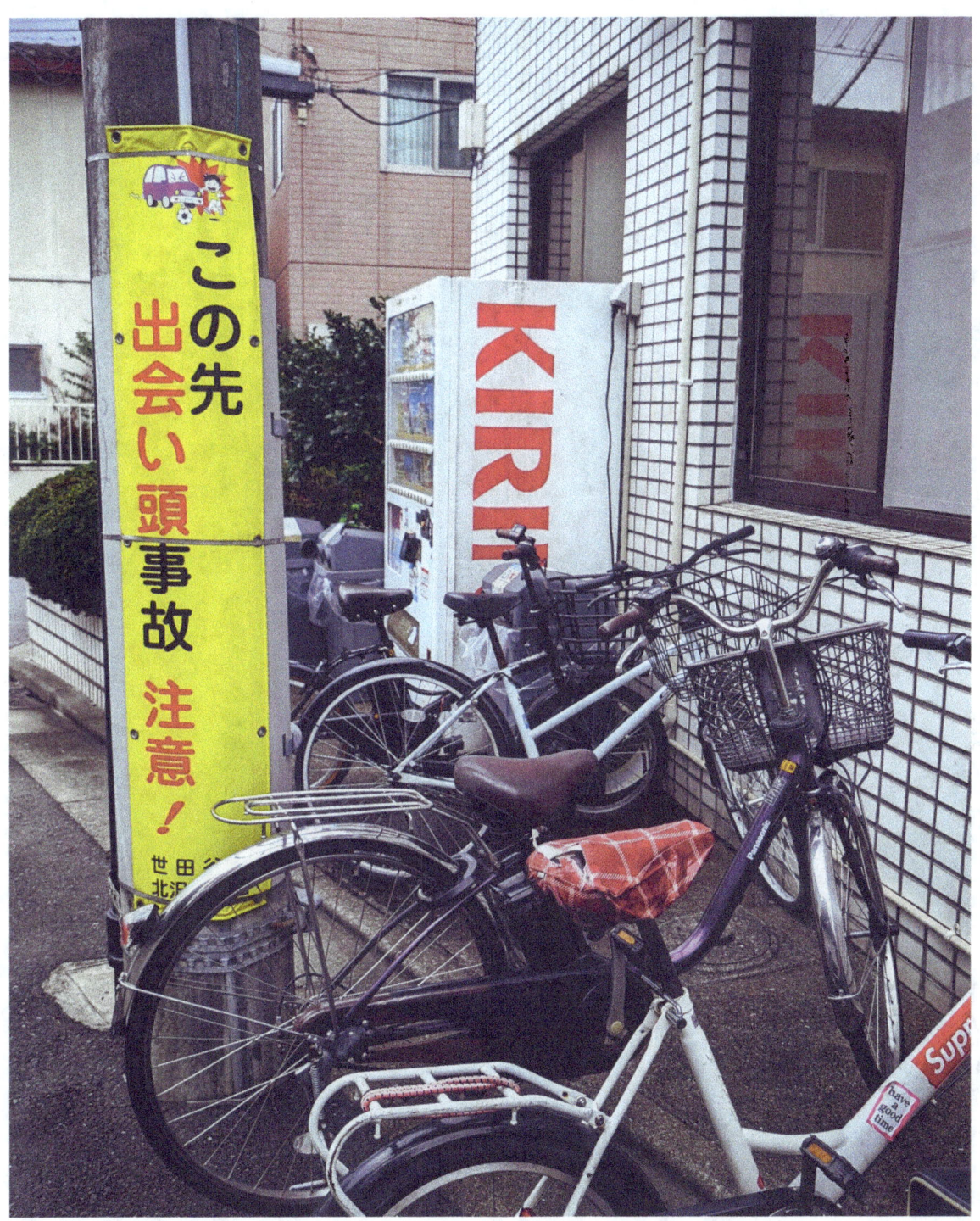

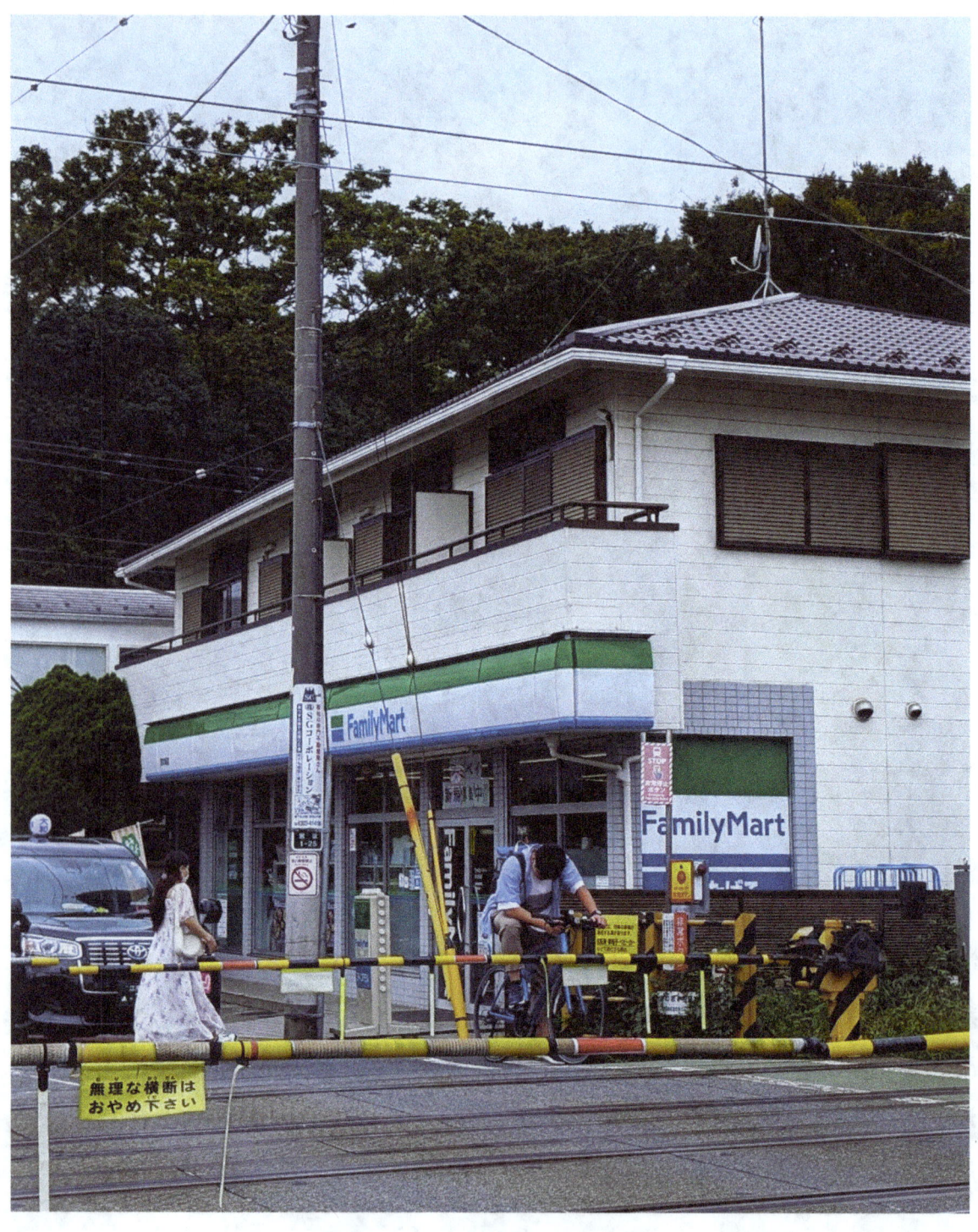

The kombini as part of the landscape and the scenery.

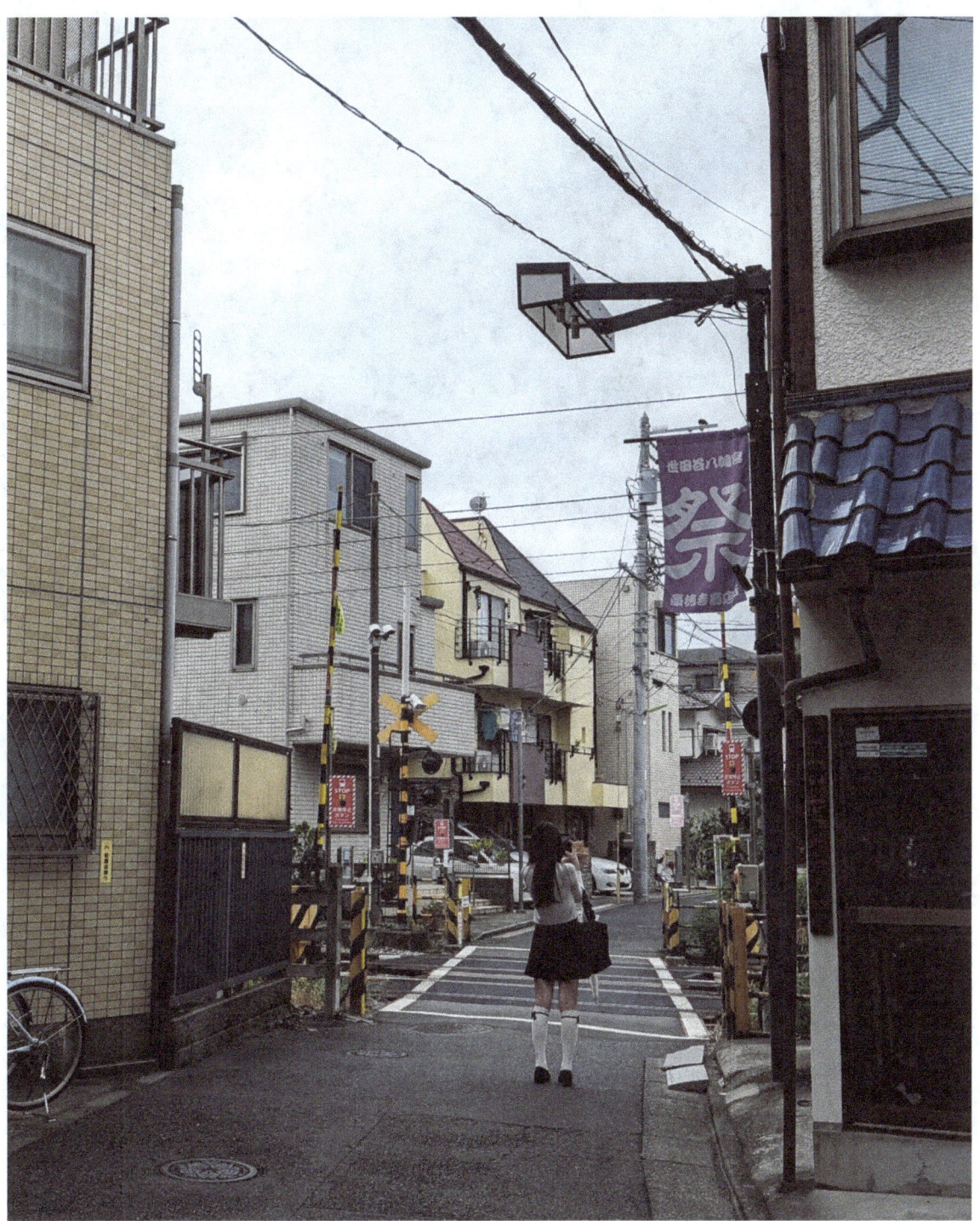

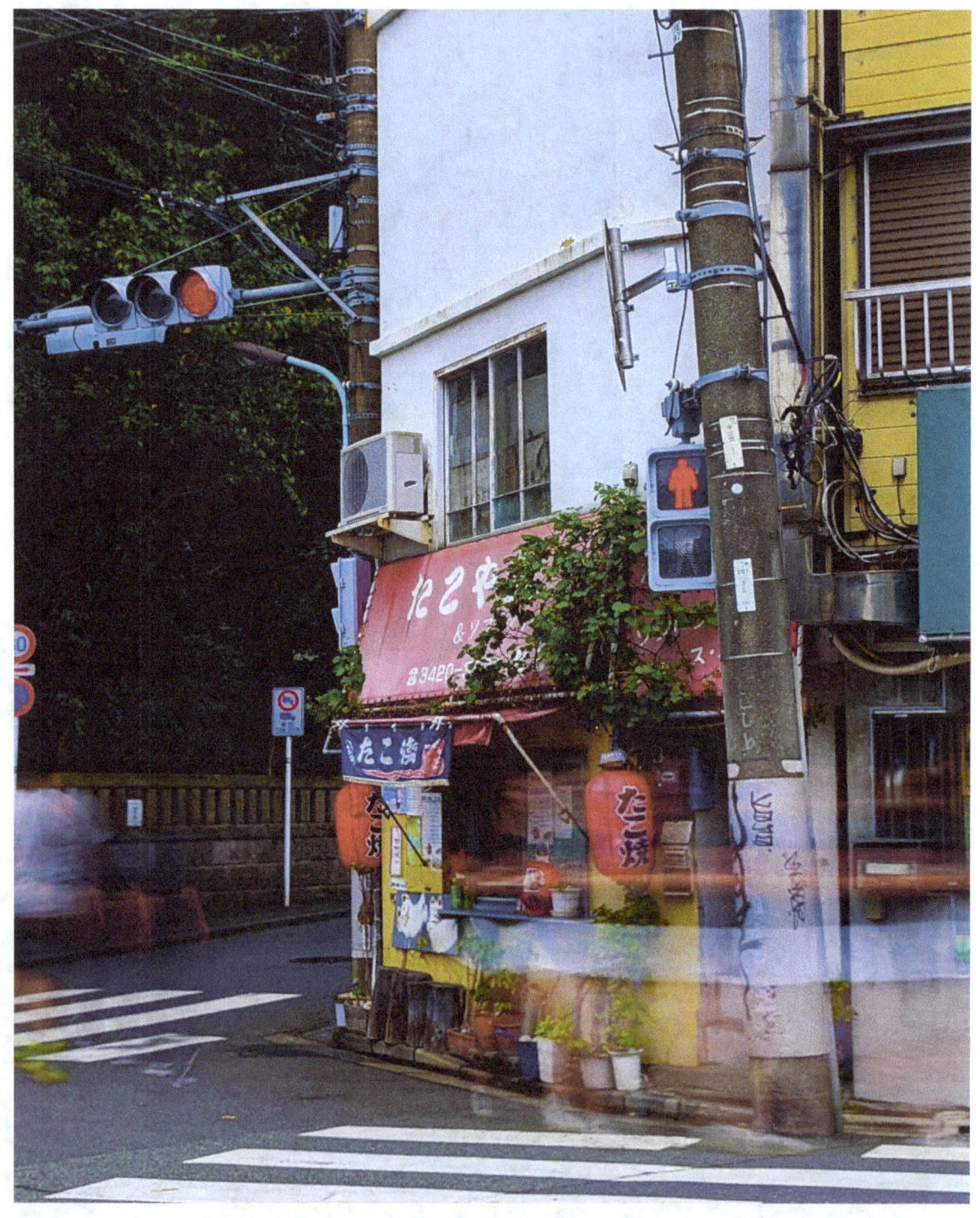

I'm captivated by every corner, with its details, its objects, those that no one touches, that everyone respects.

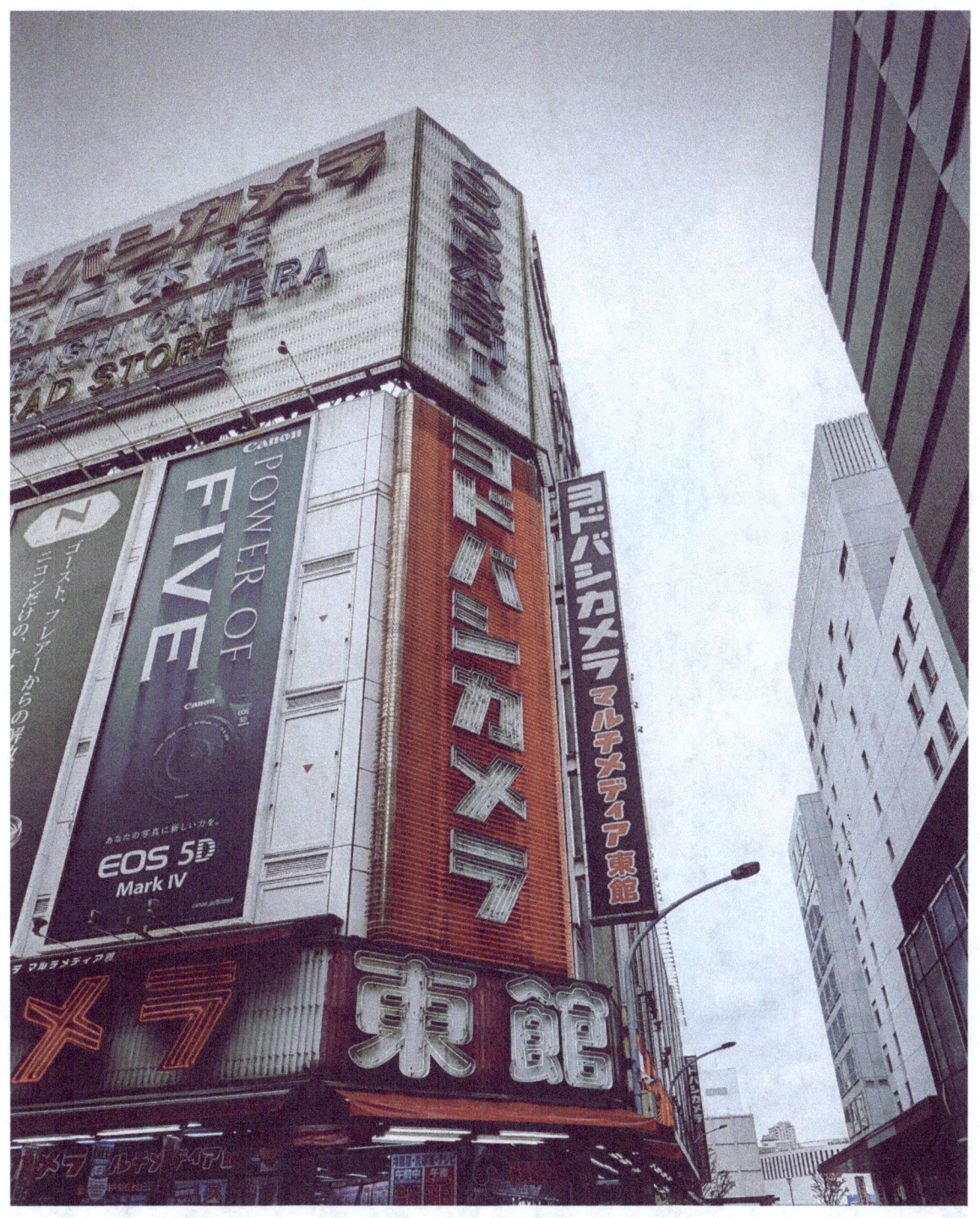

Shinjuku on a gray day, giving the area a Blade Runner-like atmosphere.

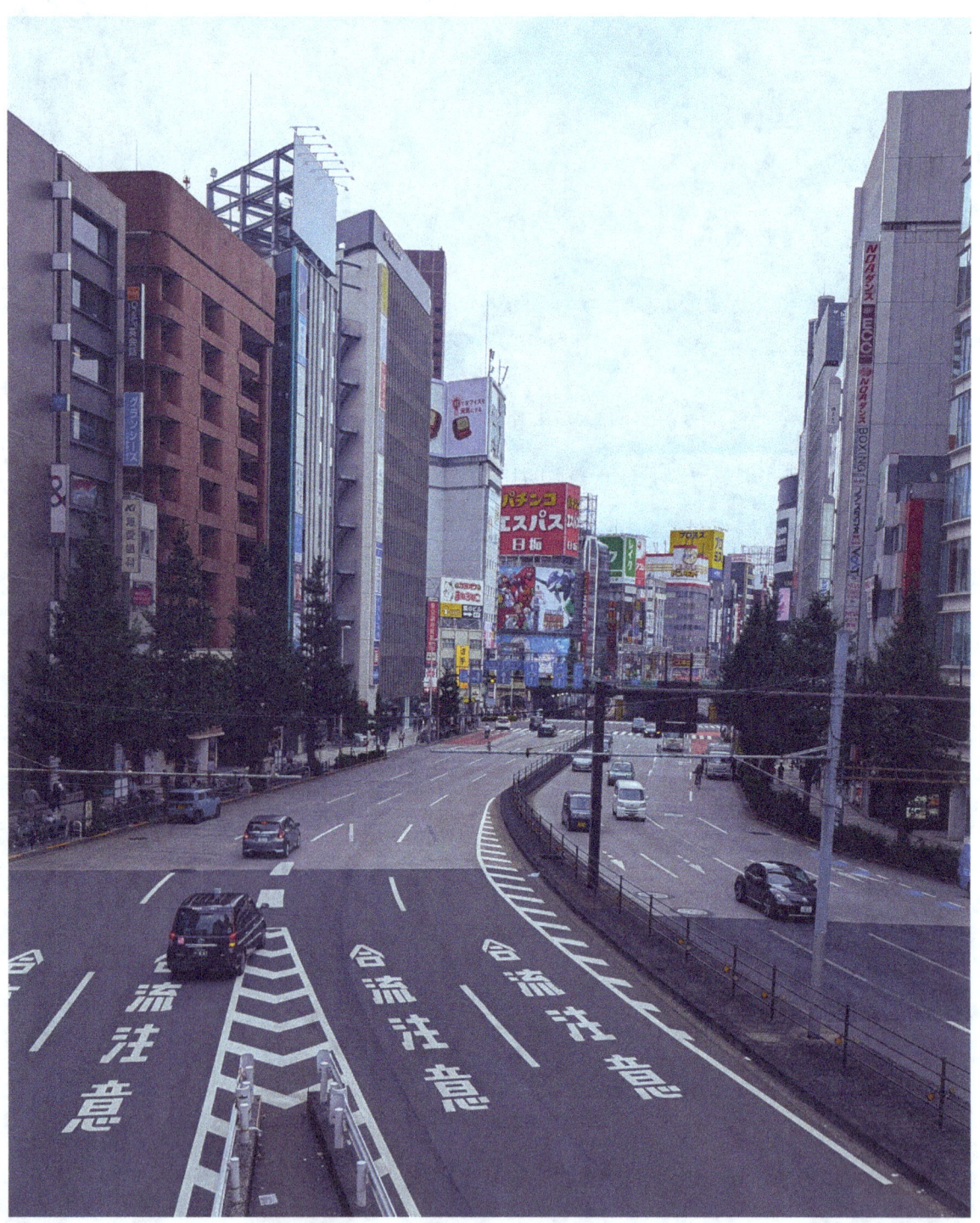

The dancing ocean of people in Shibuya.

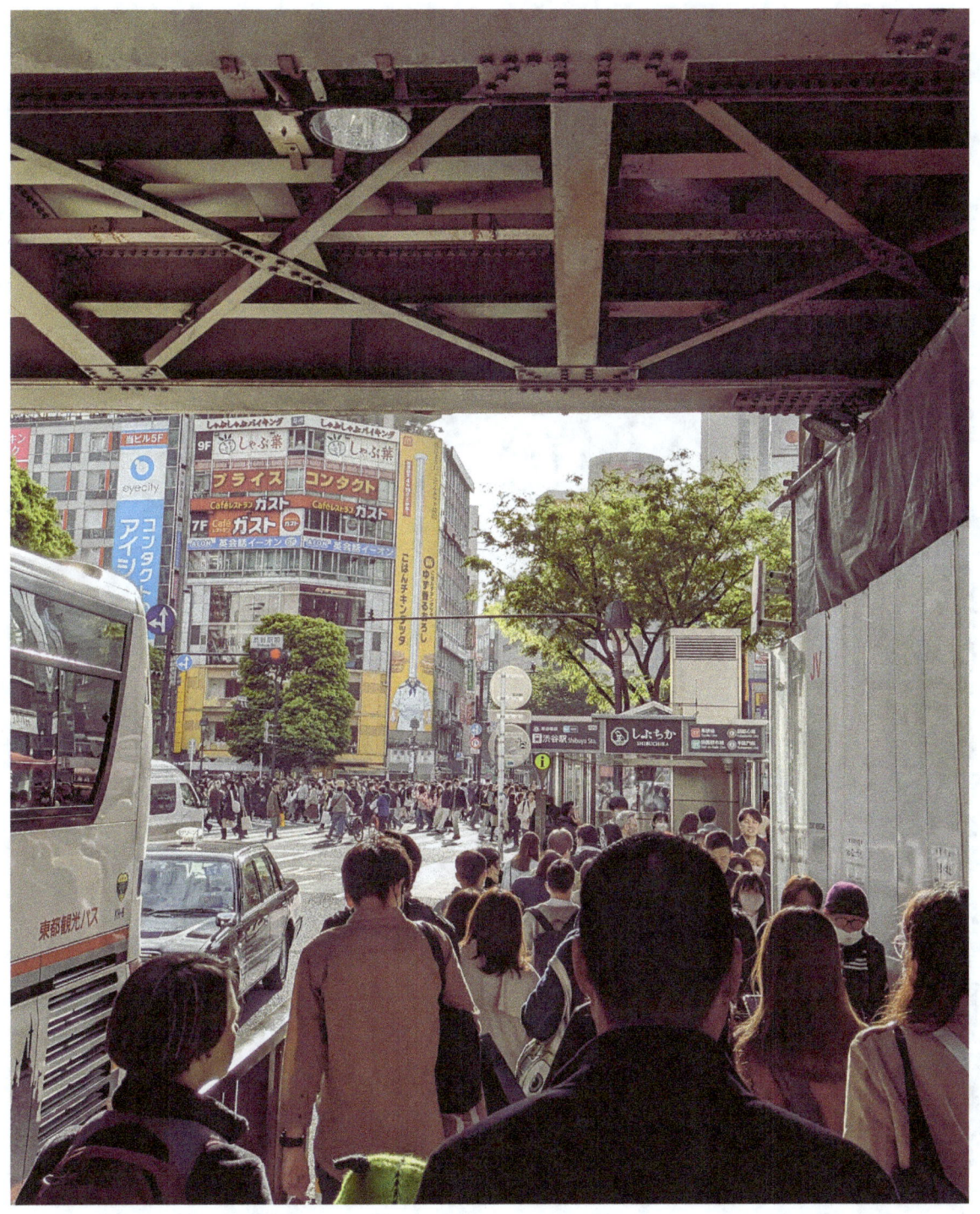

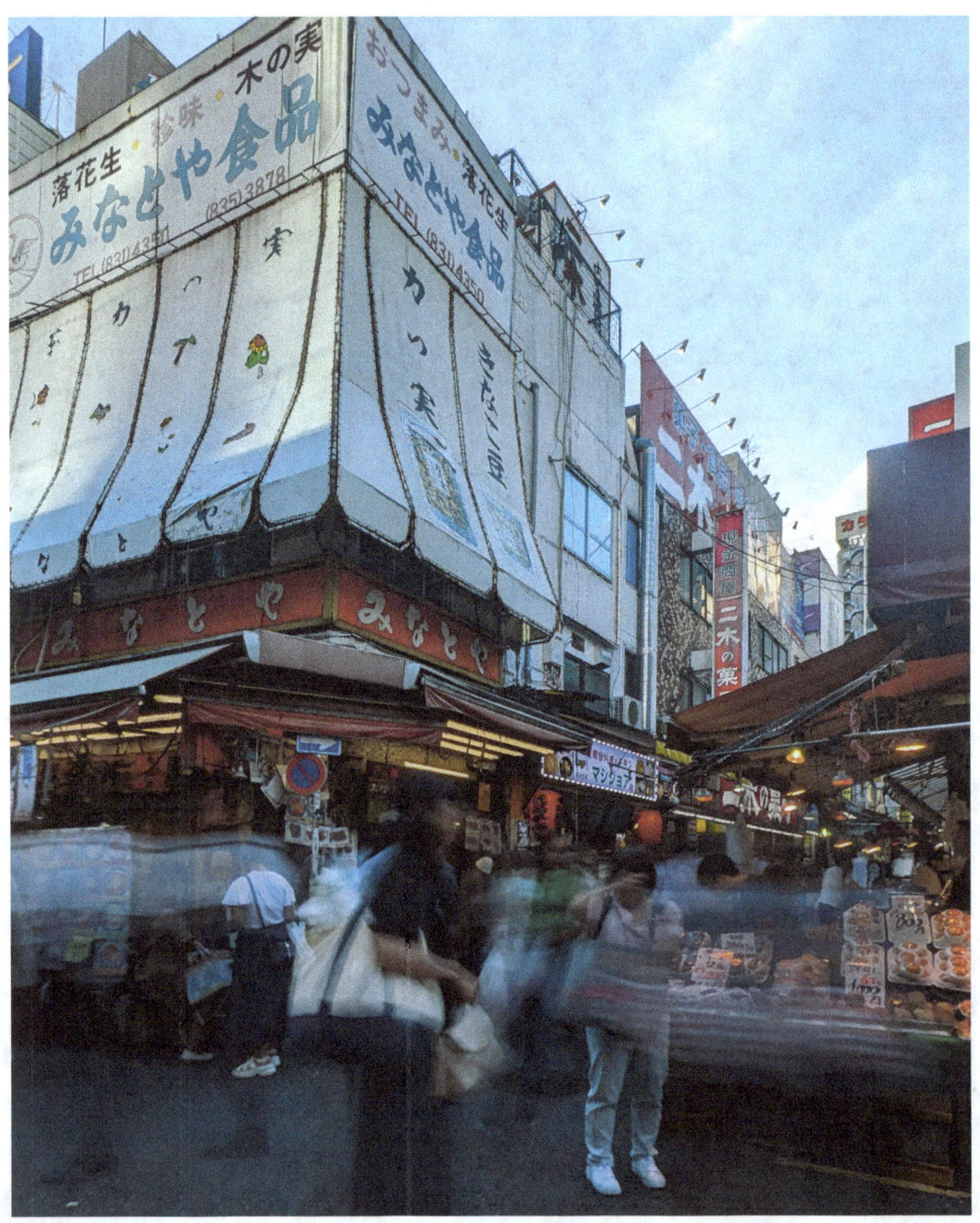

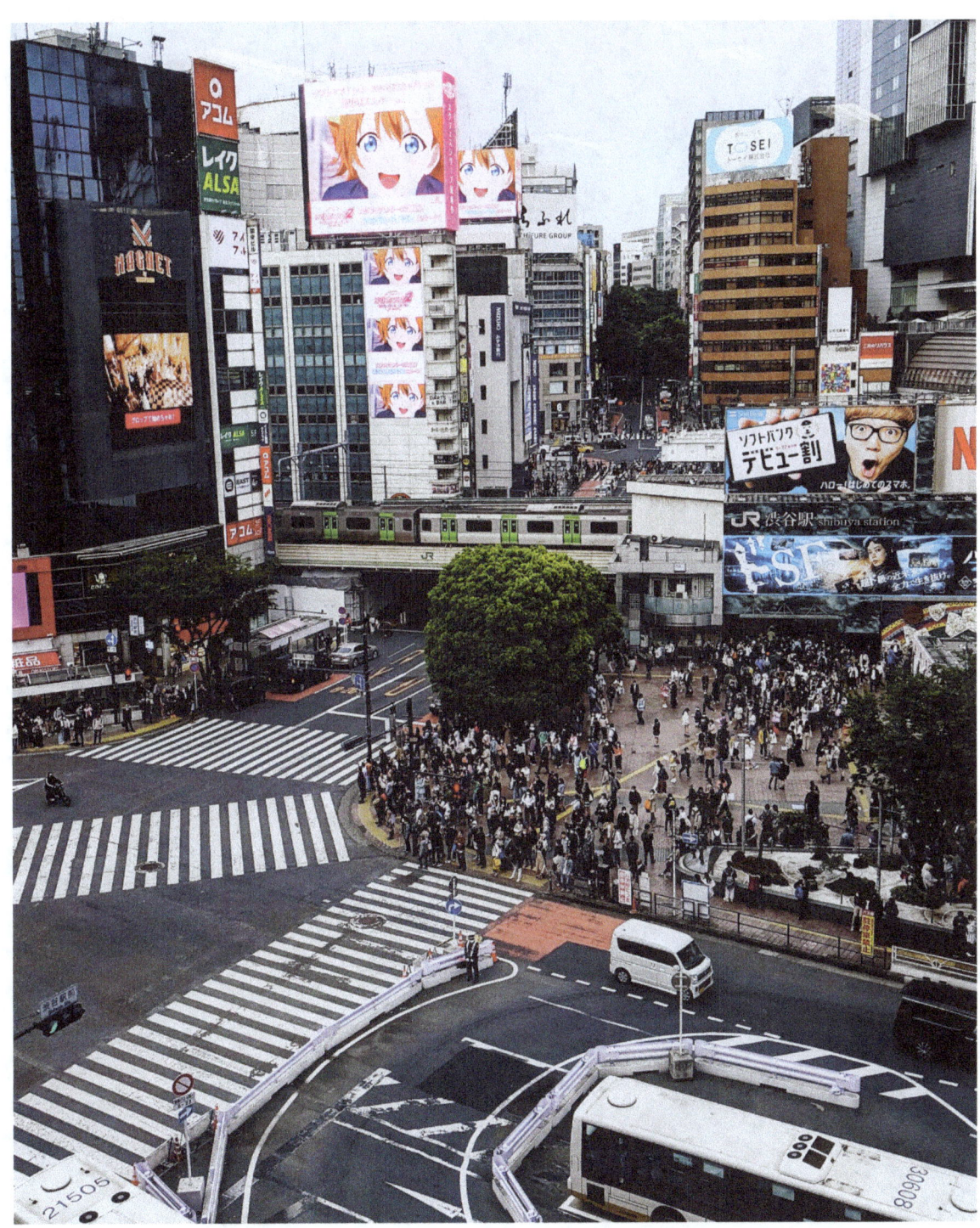

THE NIGHT

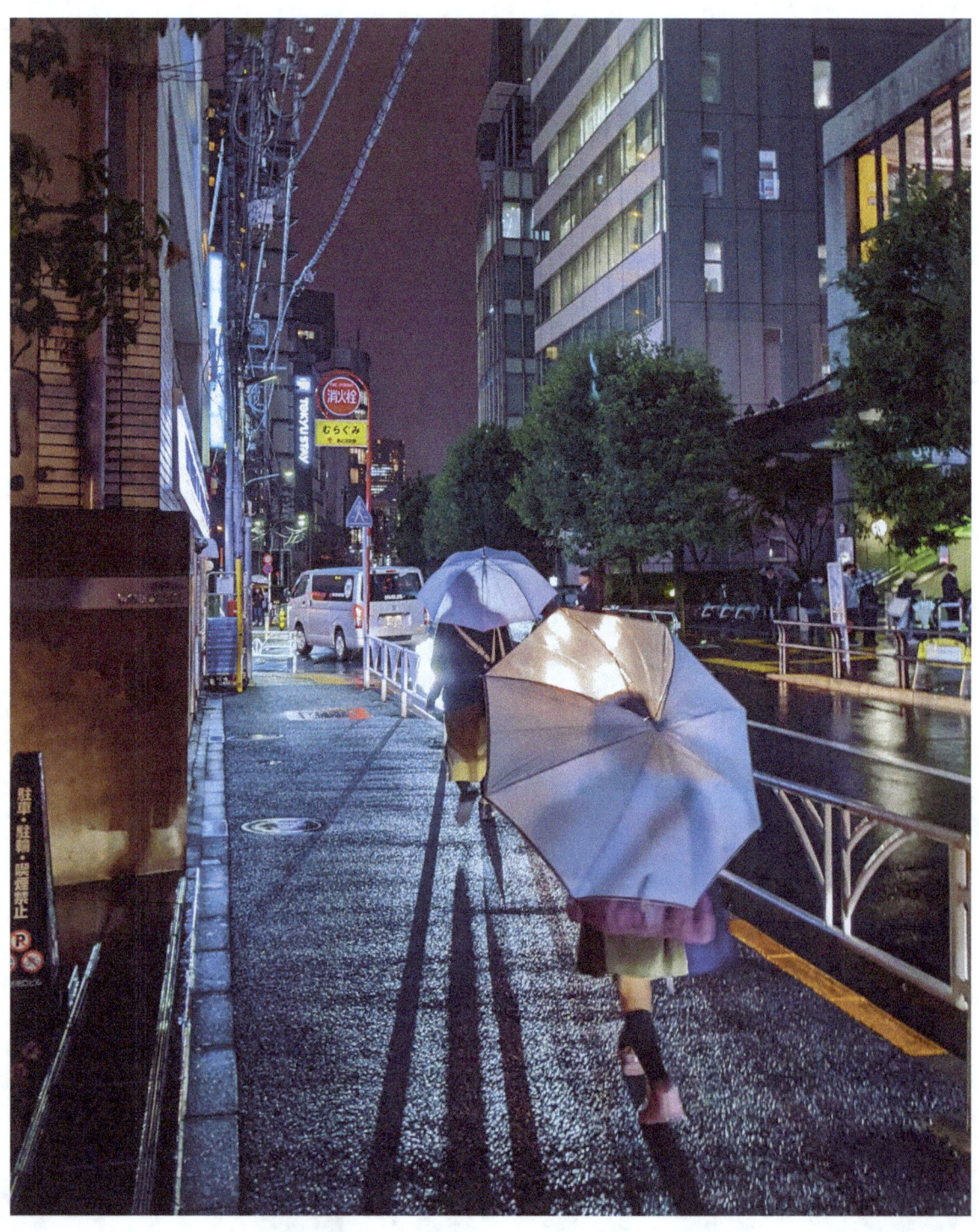

The flashes of the wet pavement create a spectacular scene of bright and colorful lights.

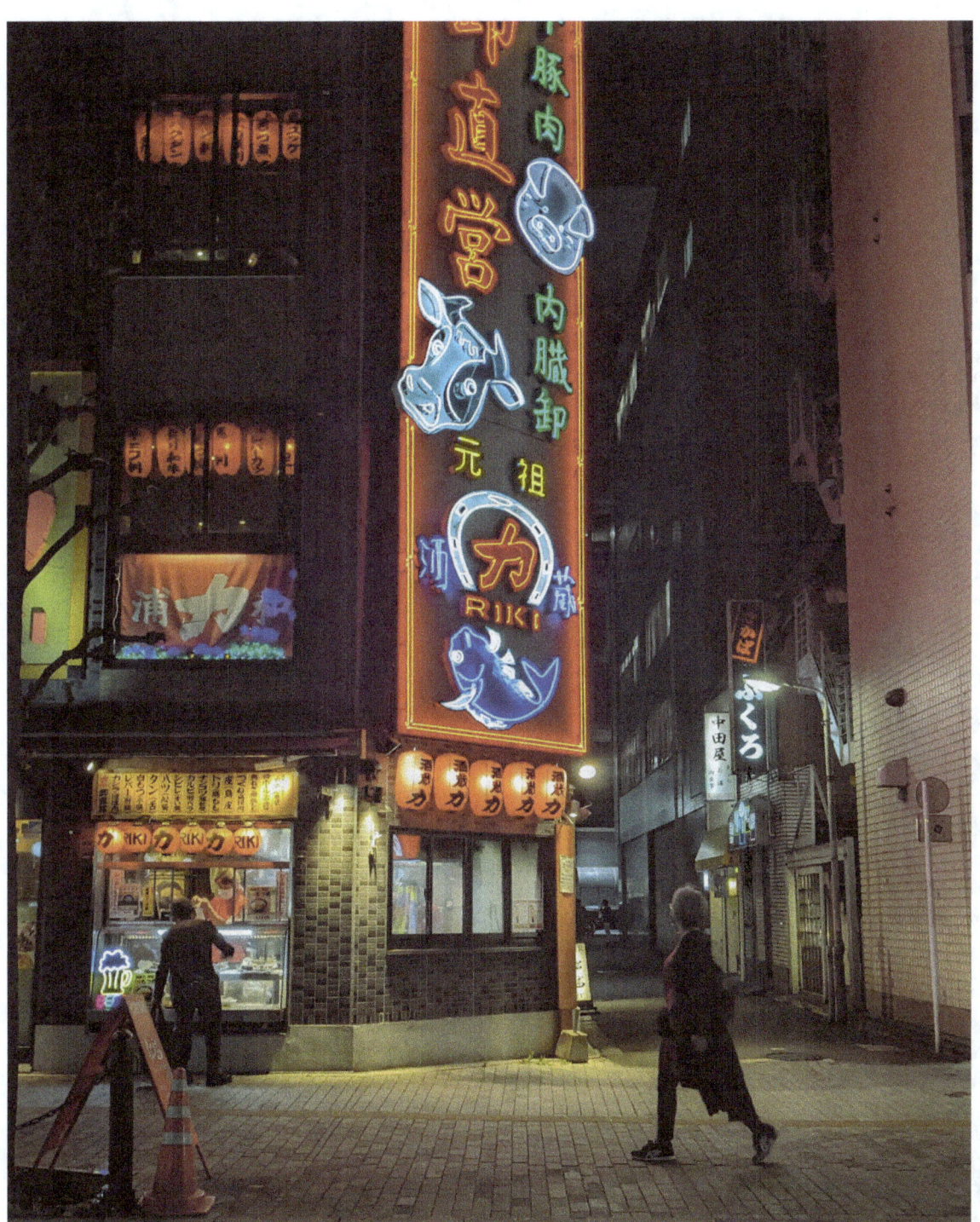

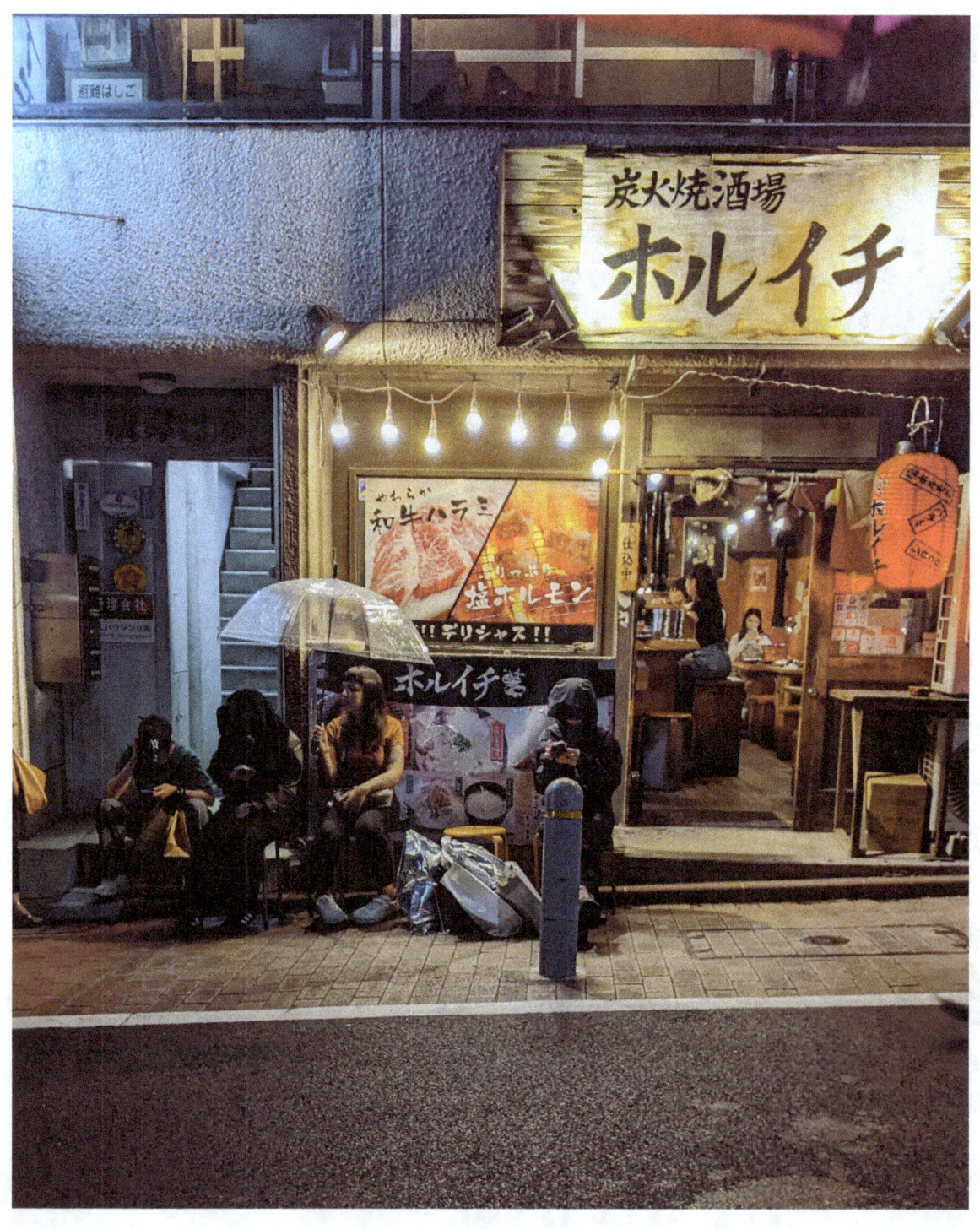

That night, we waited an hour under the light rain, embraced by the warm breeze and the aroma of wagyu.

This image stopped me from walking, I wanted to make that moment, that child, immortal.

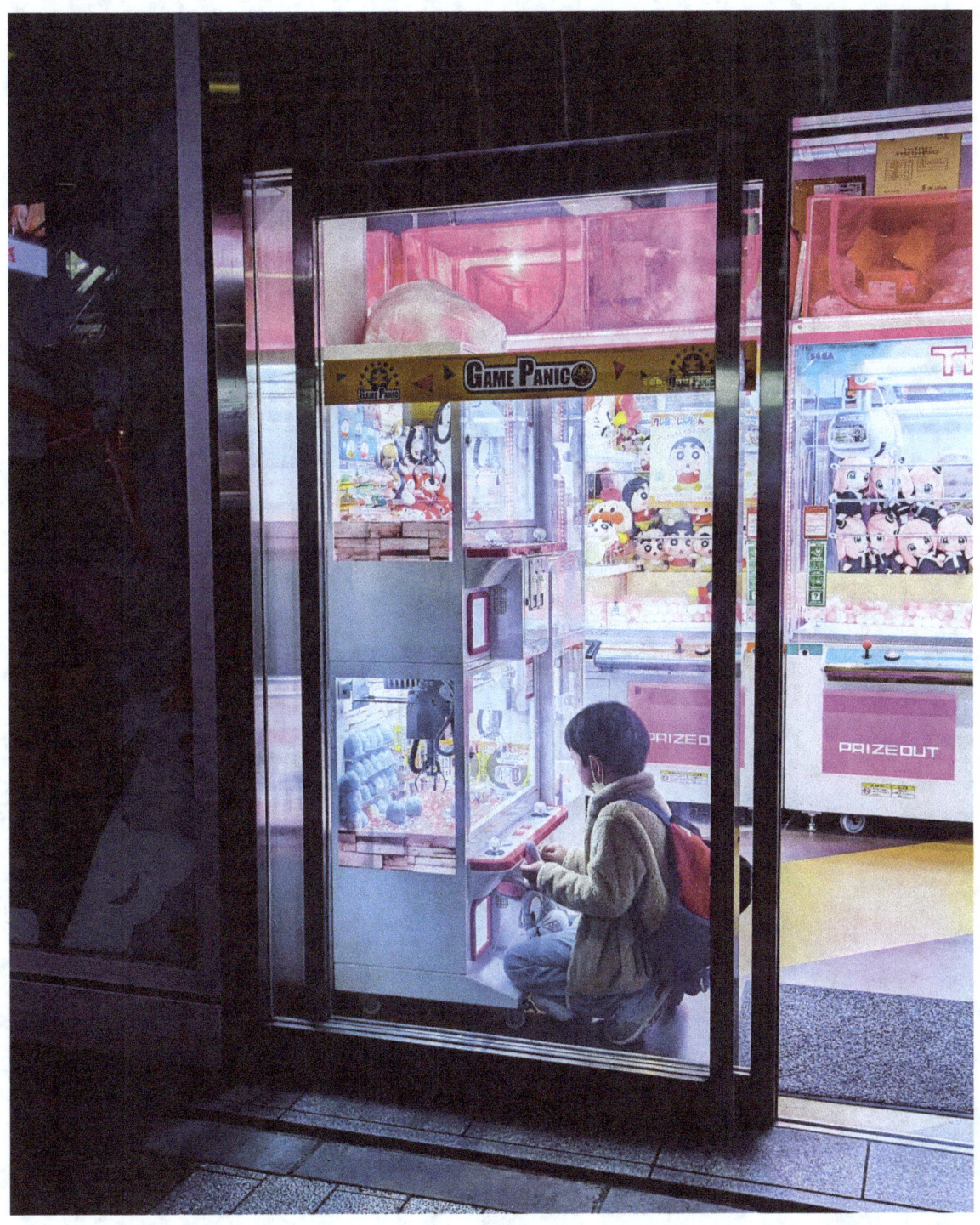

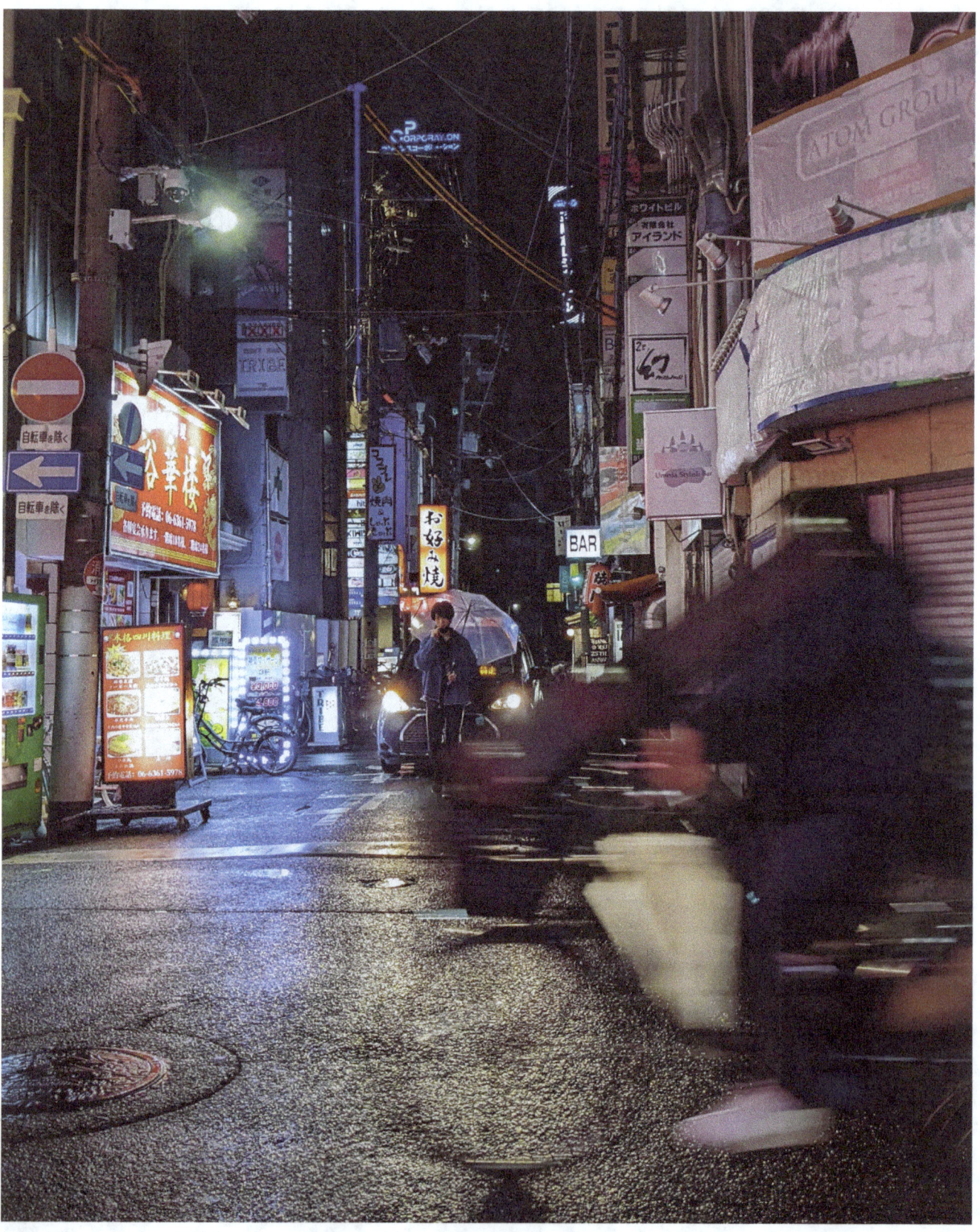

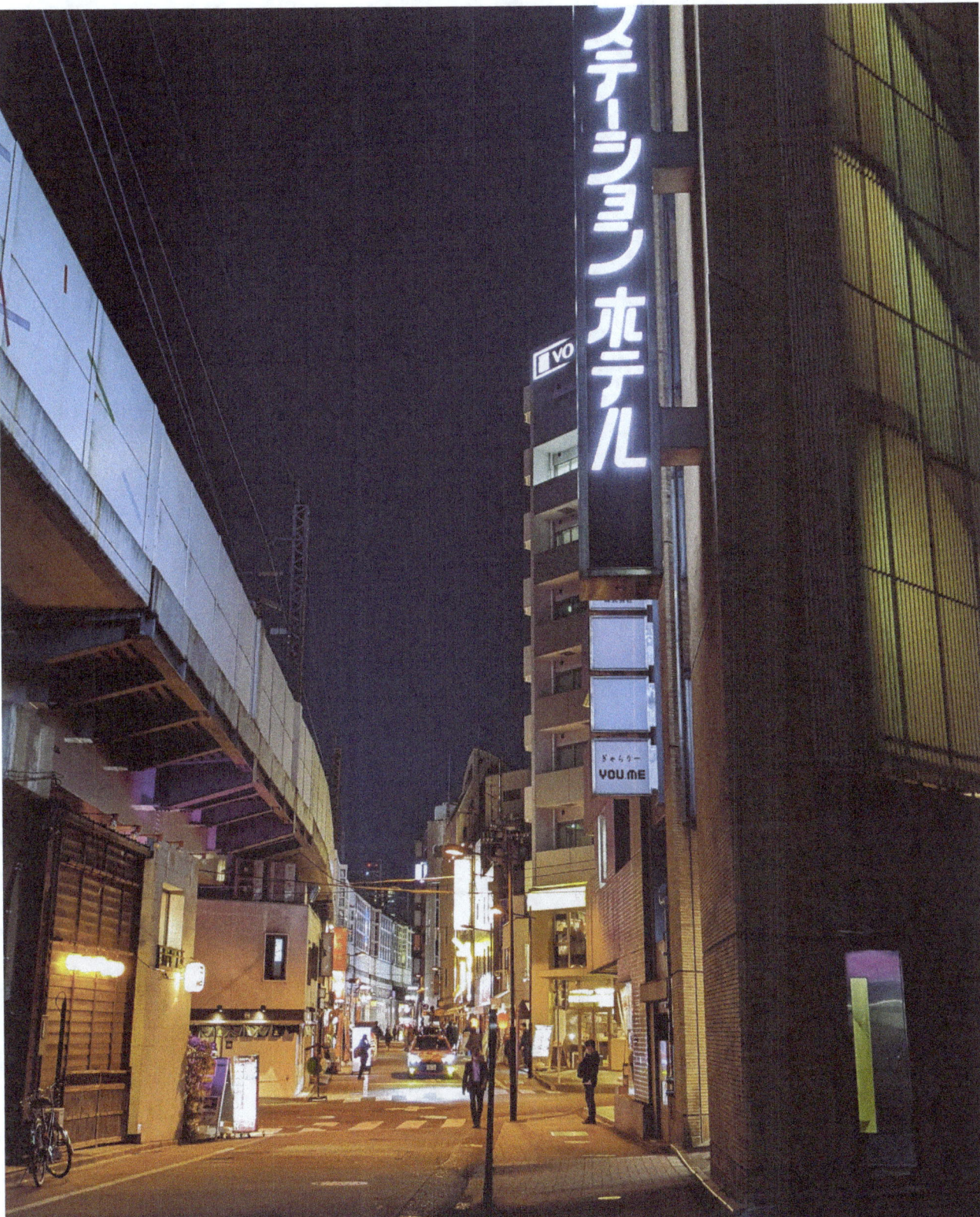

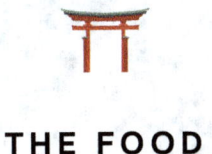

THE FOOD

They call it umami, that perfect flavor, which is the sum of all flavors.

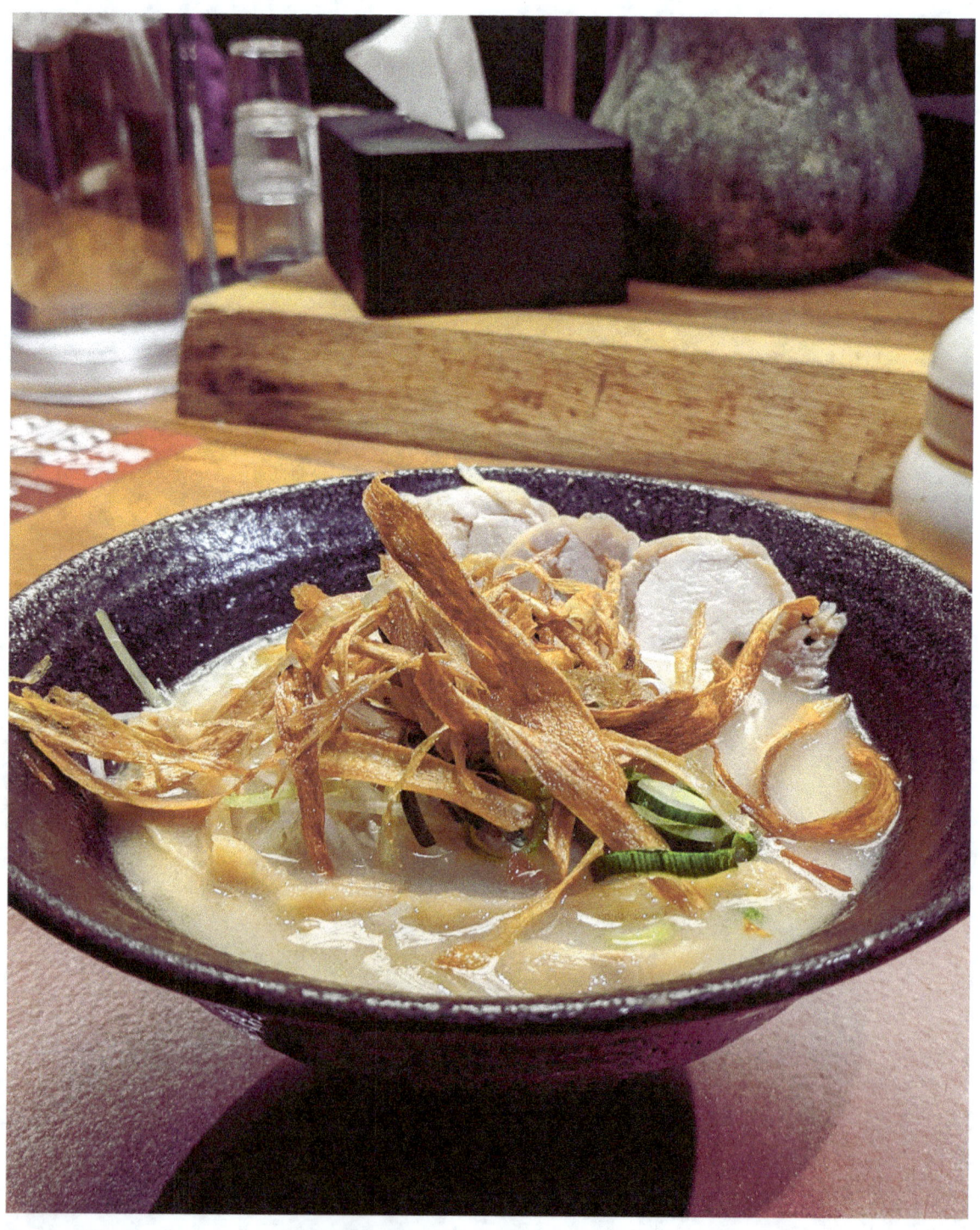

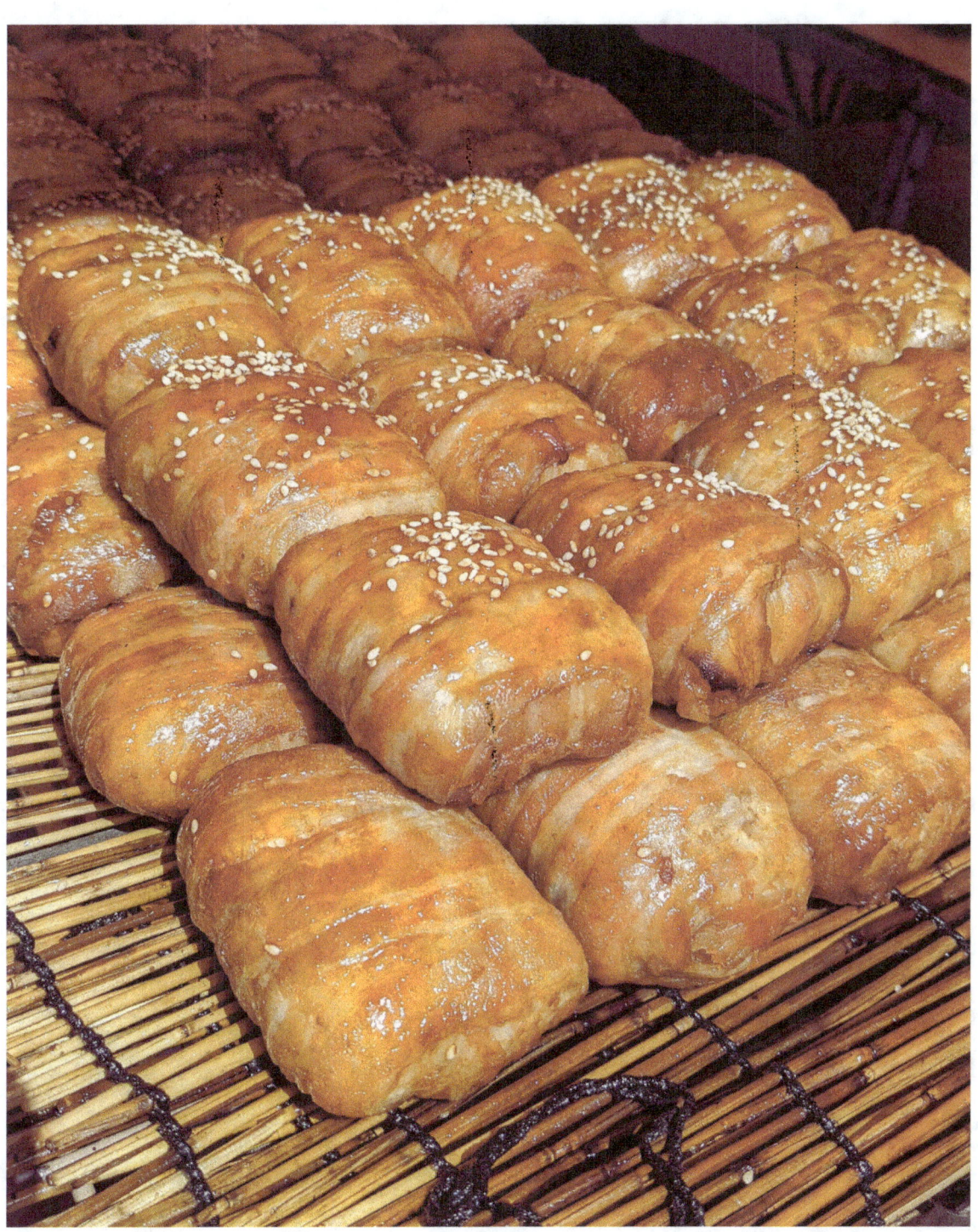

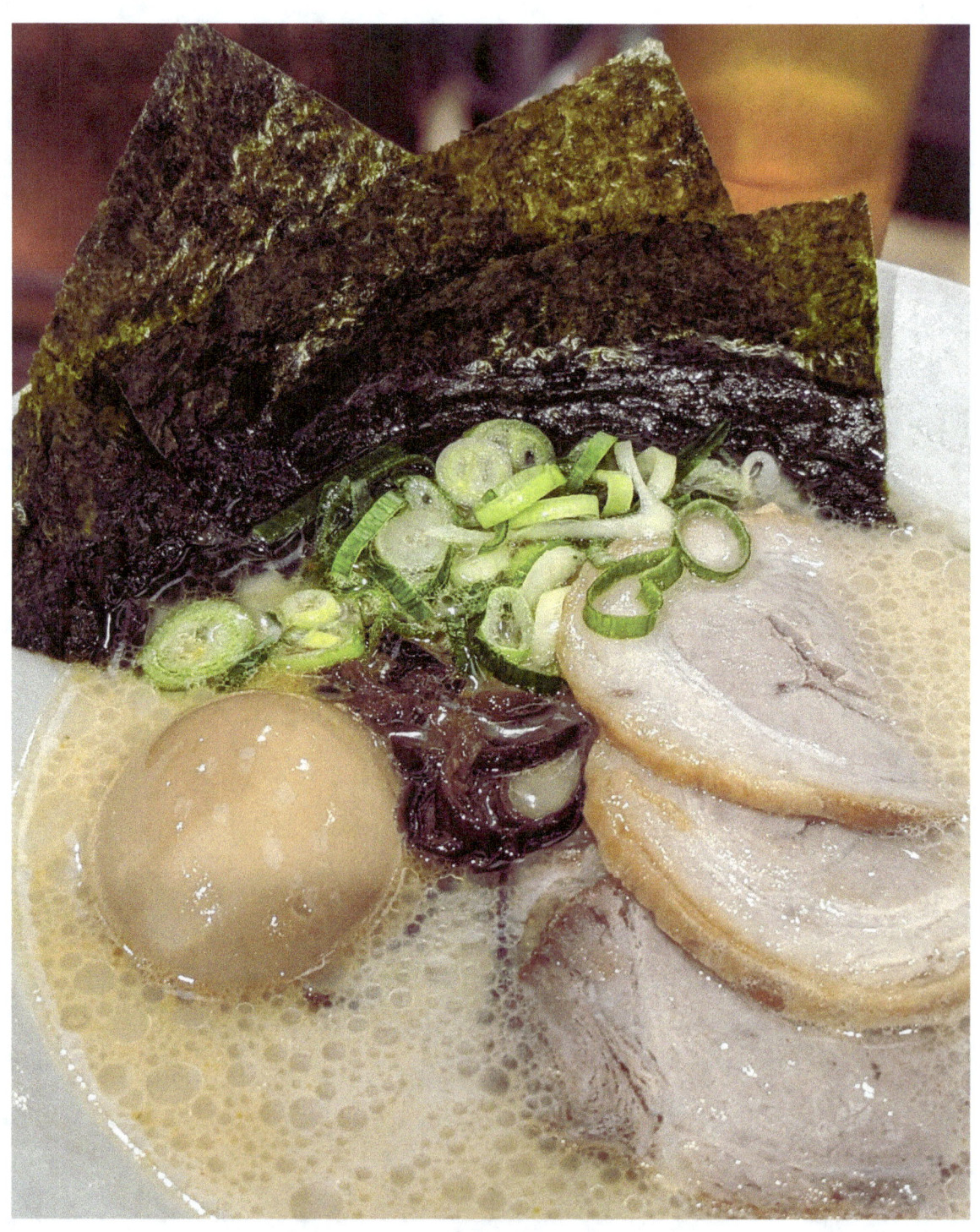

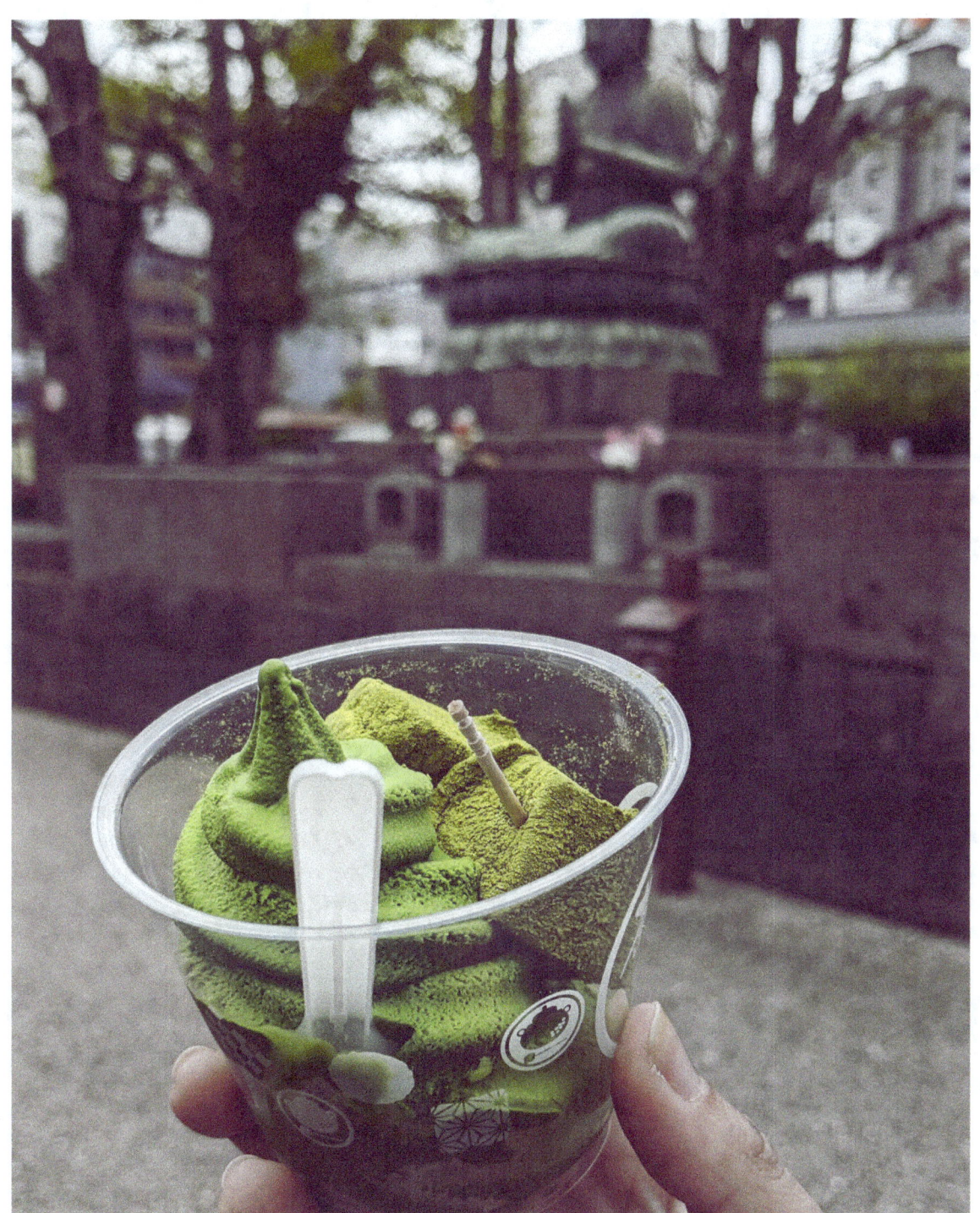

The umami of oyster broth.

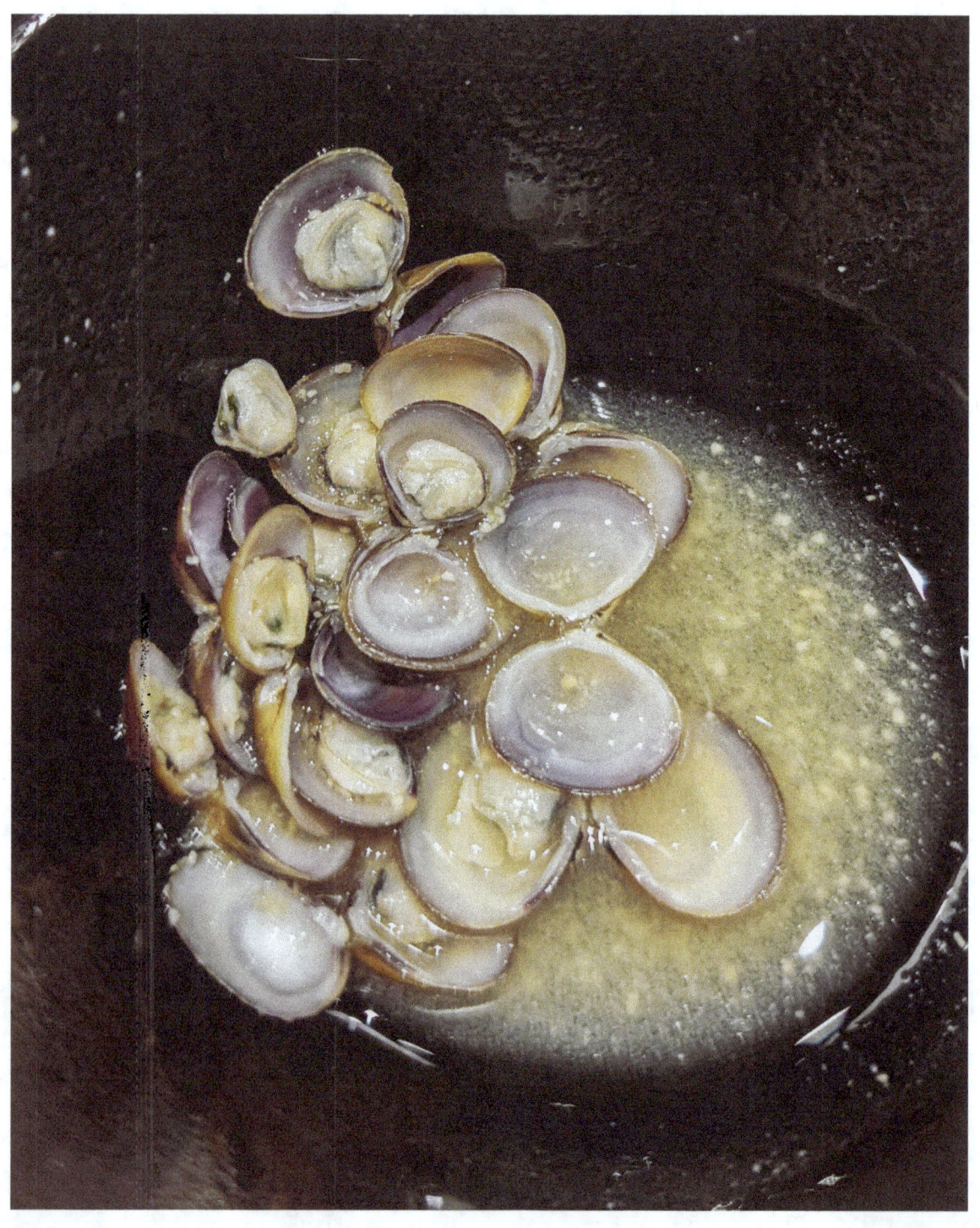

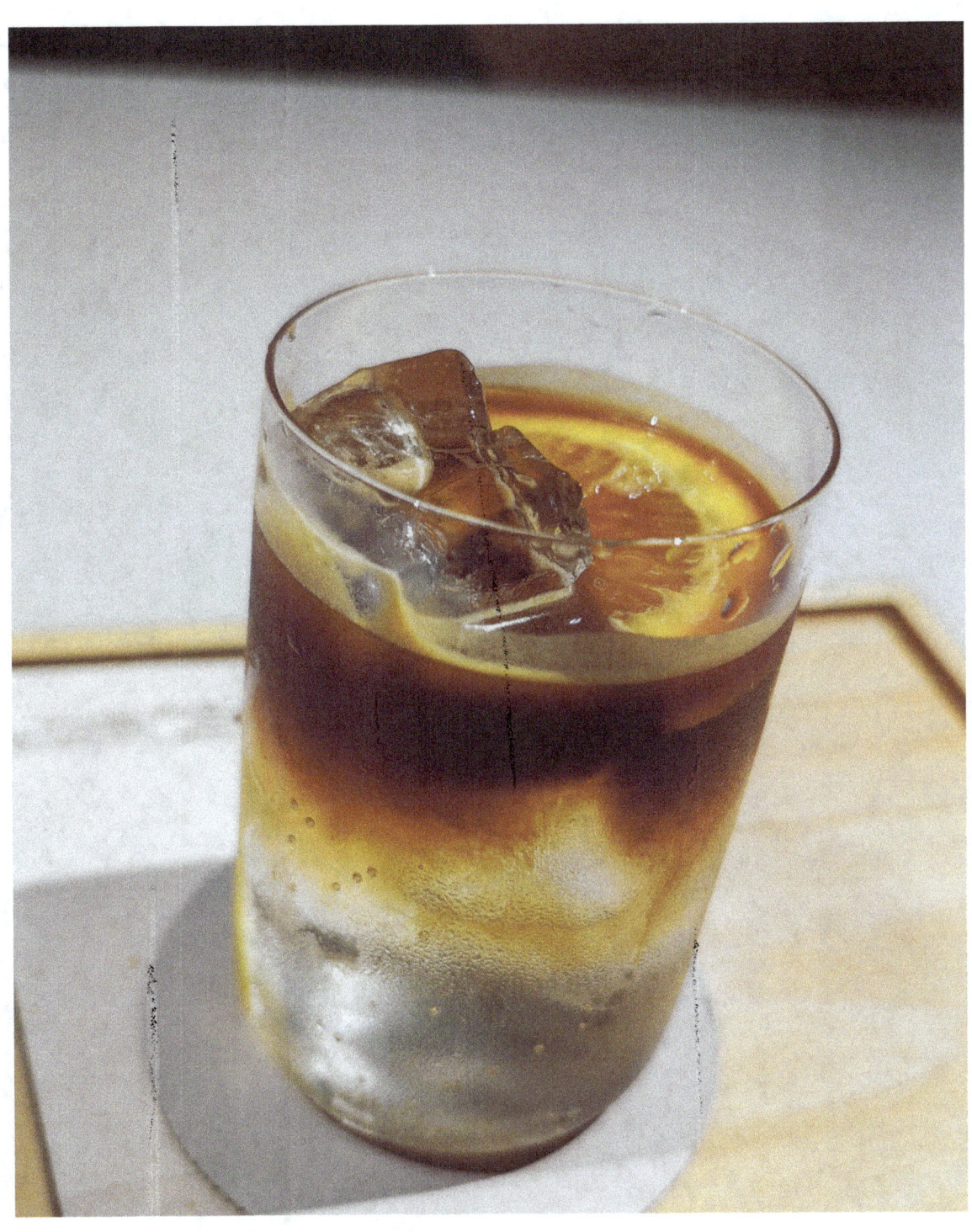
Orange tonic espresso, in a cafe in Omotesando.

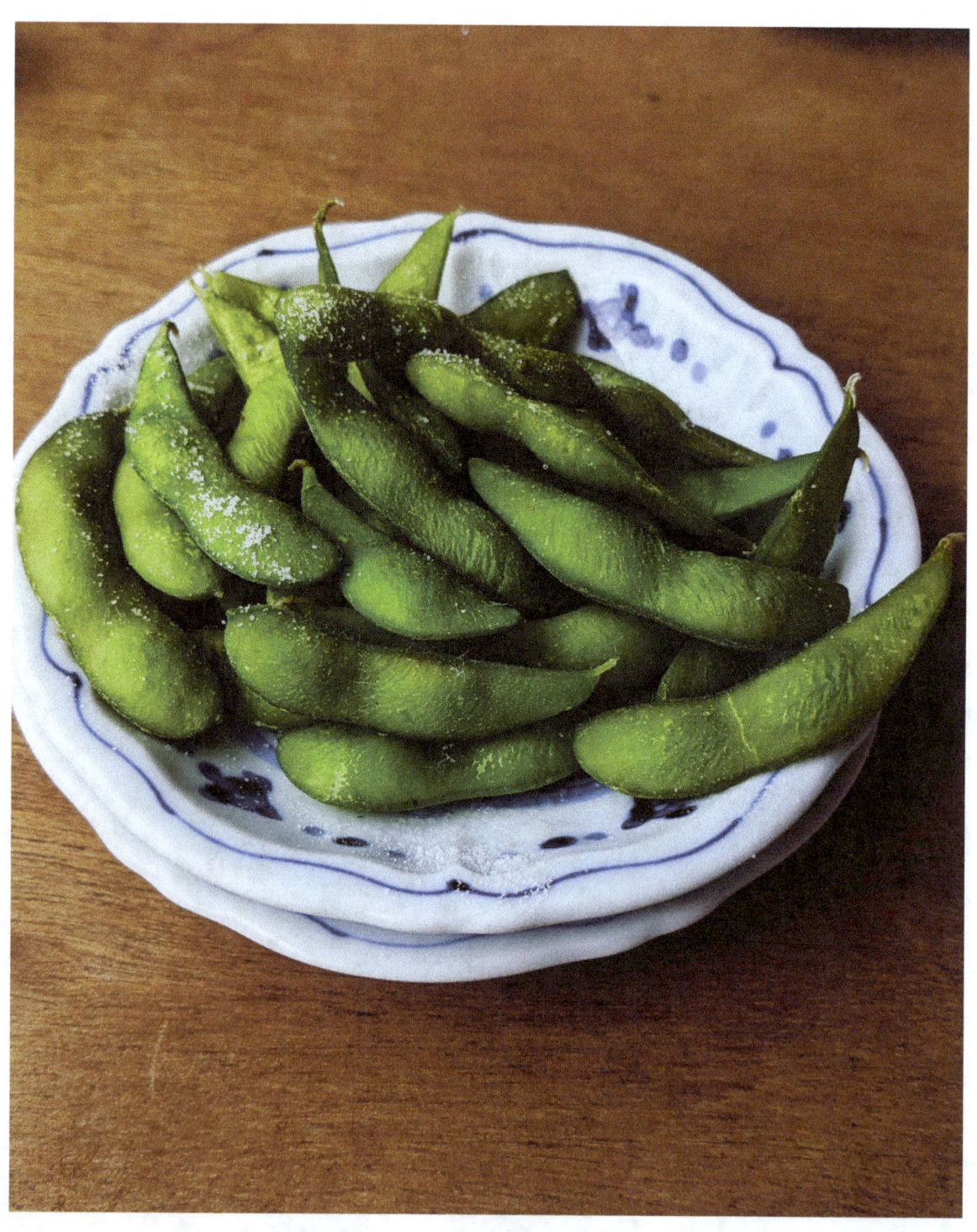

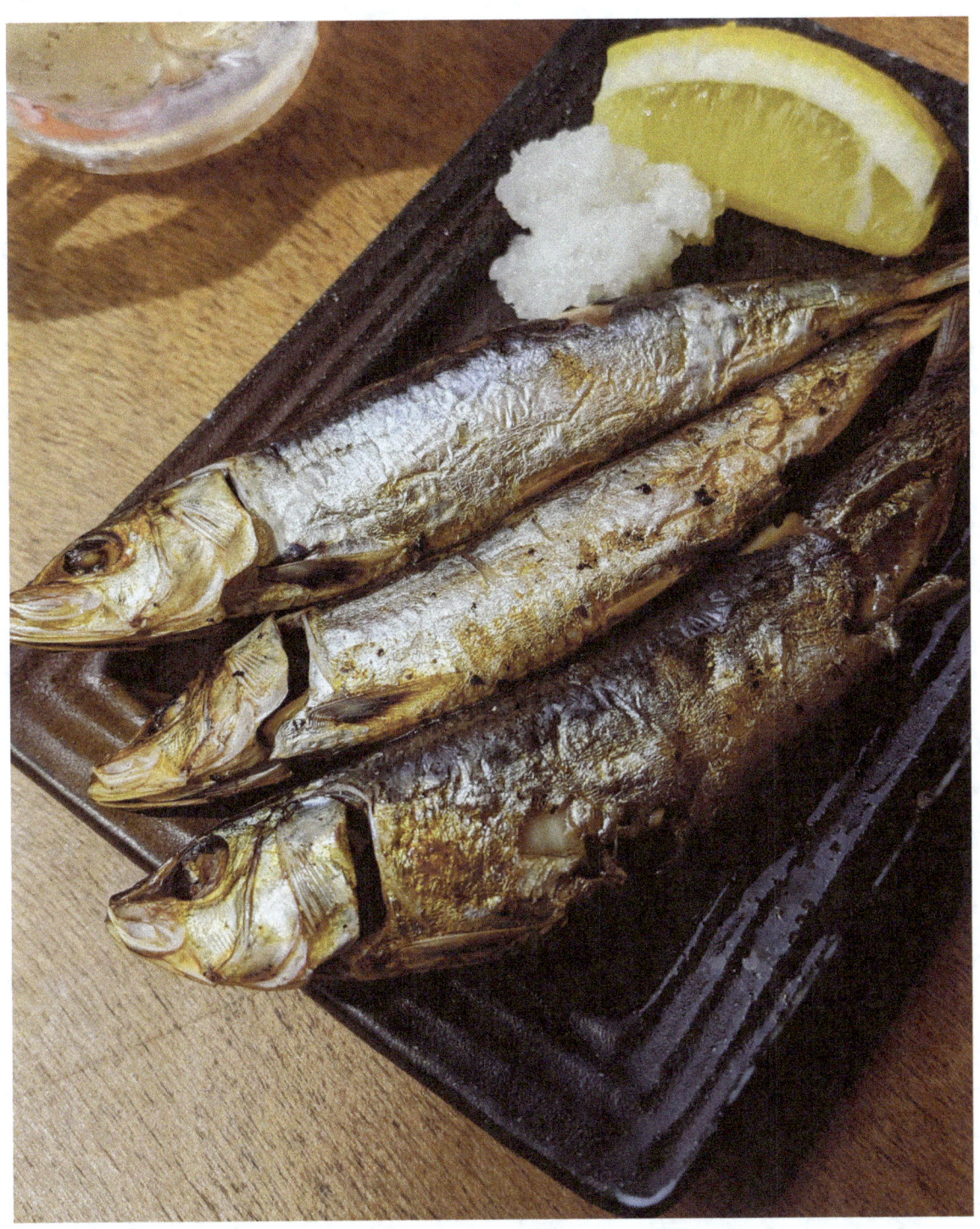

In Hiroshima, you must eat Okonomiyaki, and you must see the show.

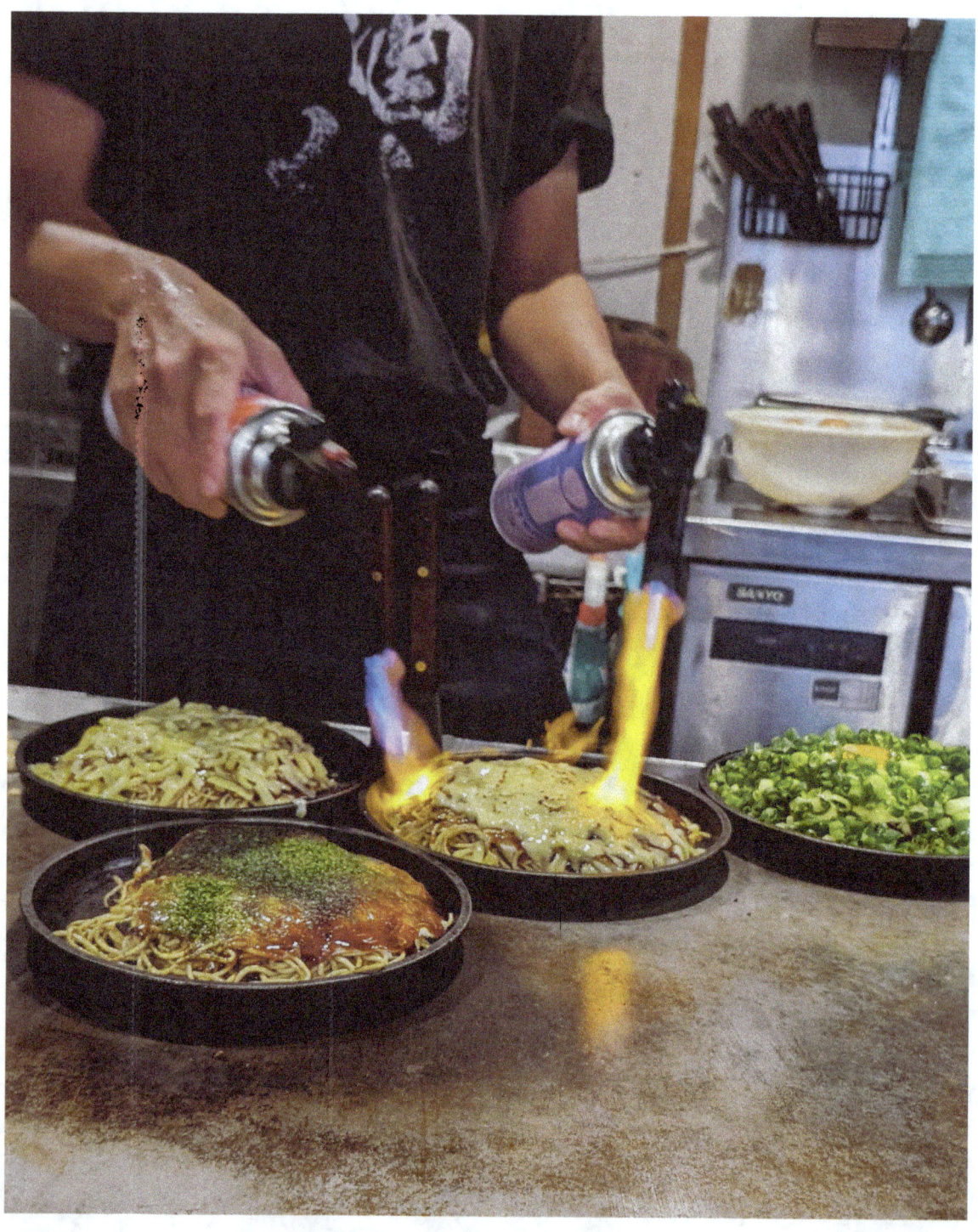

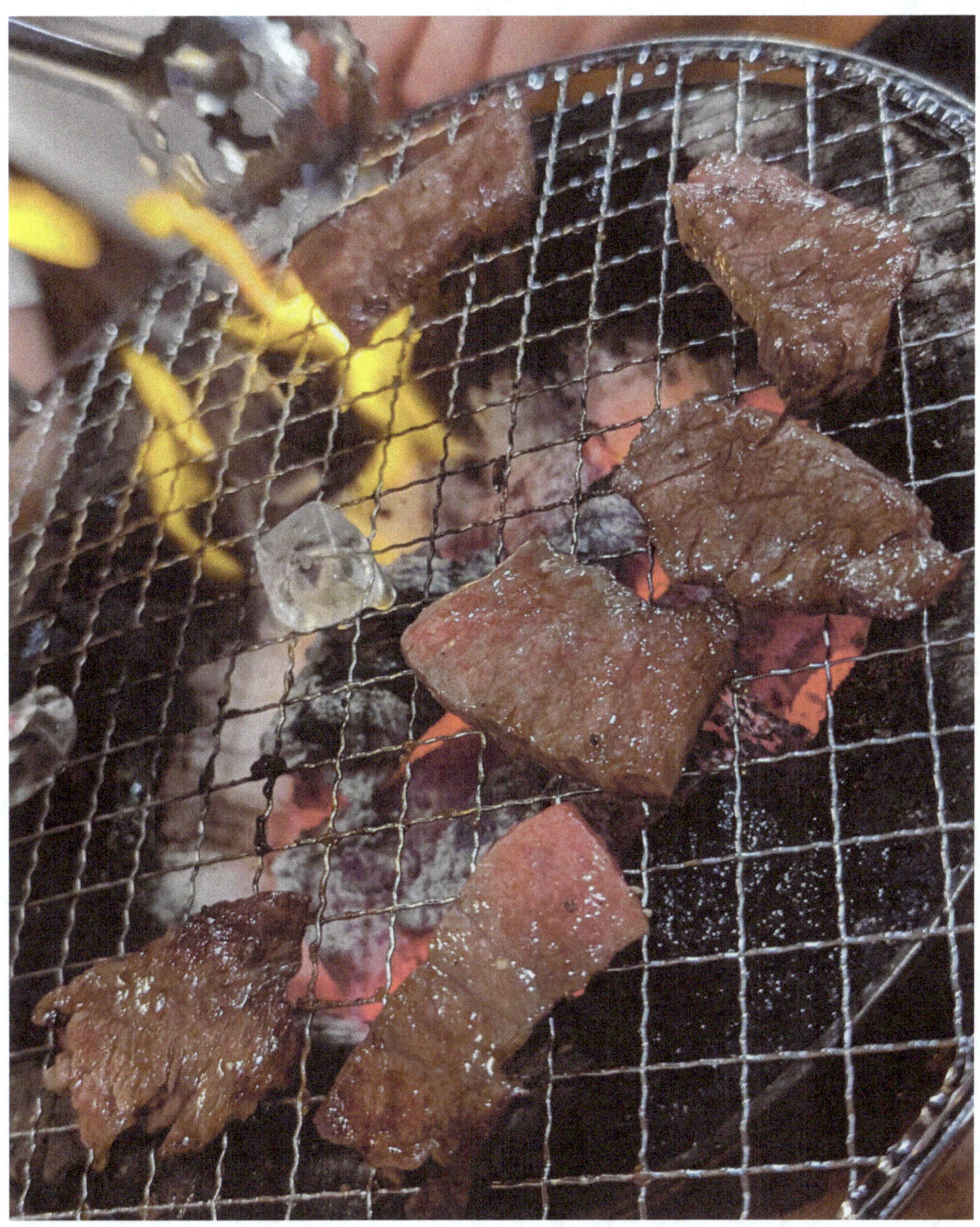

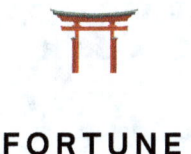

FORTUNE

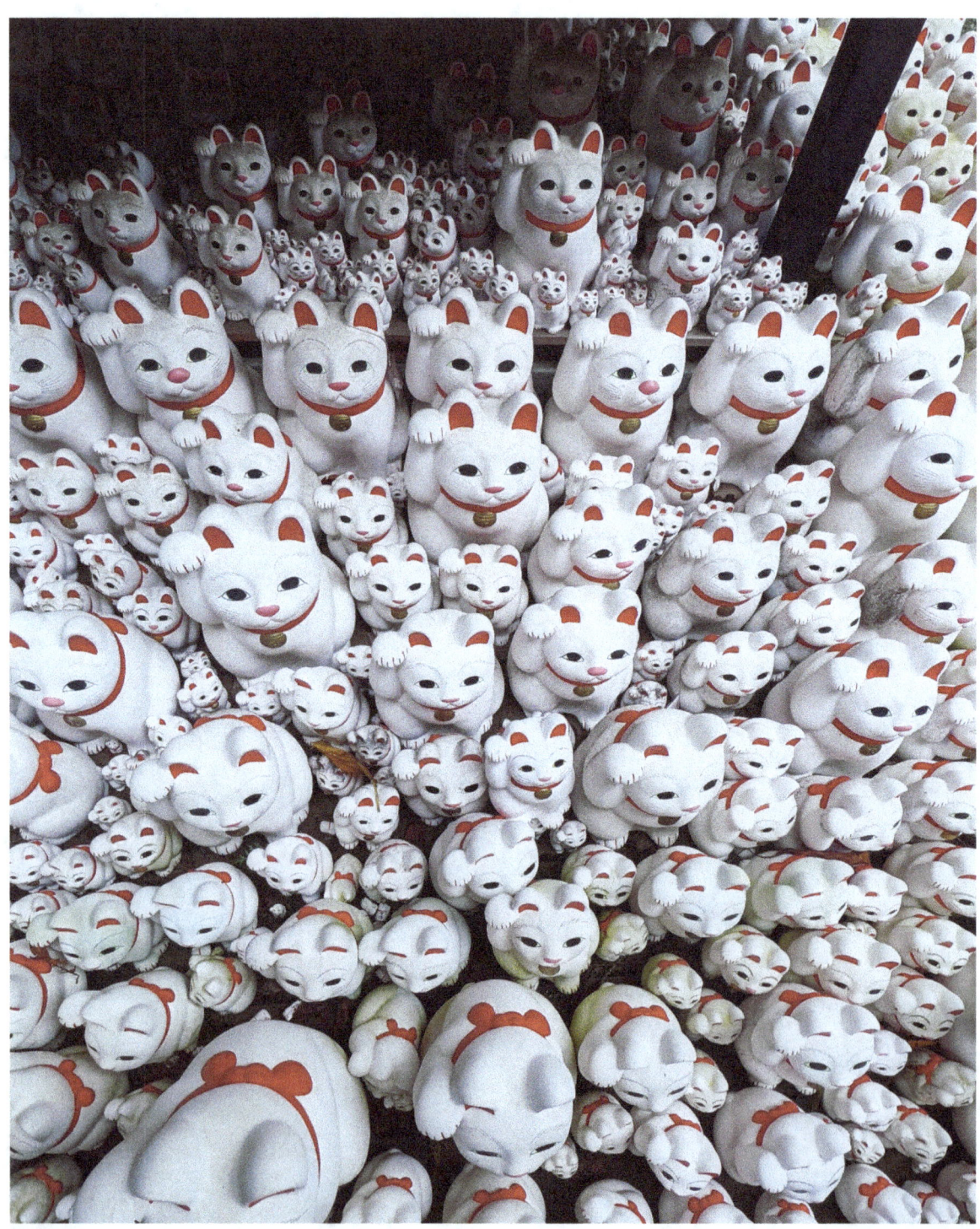

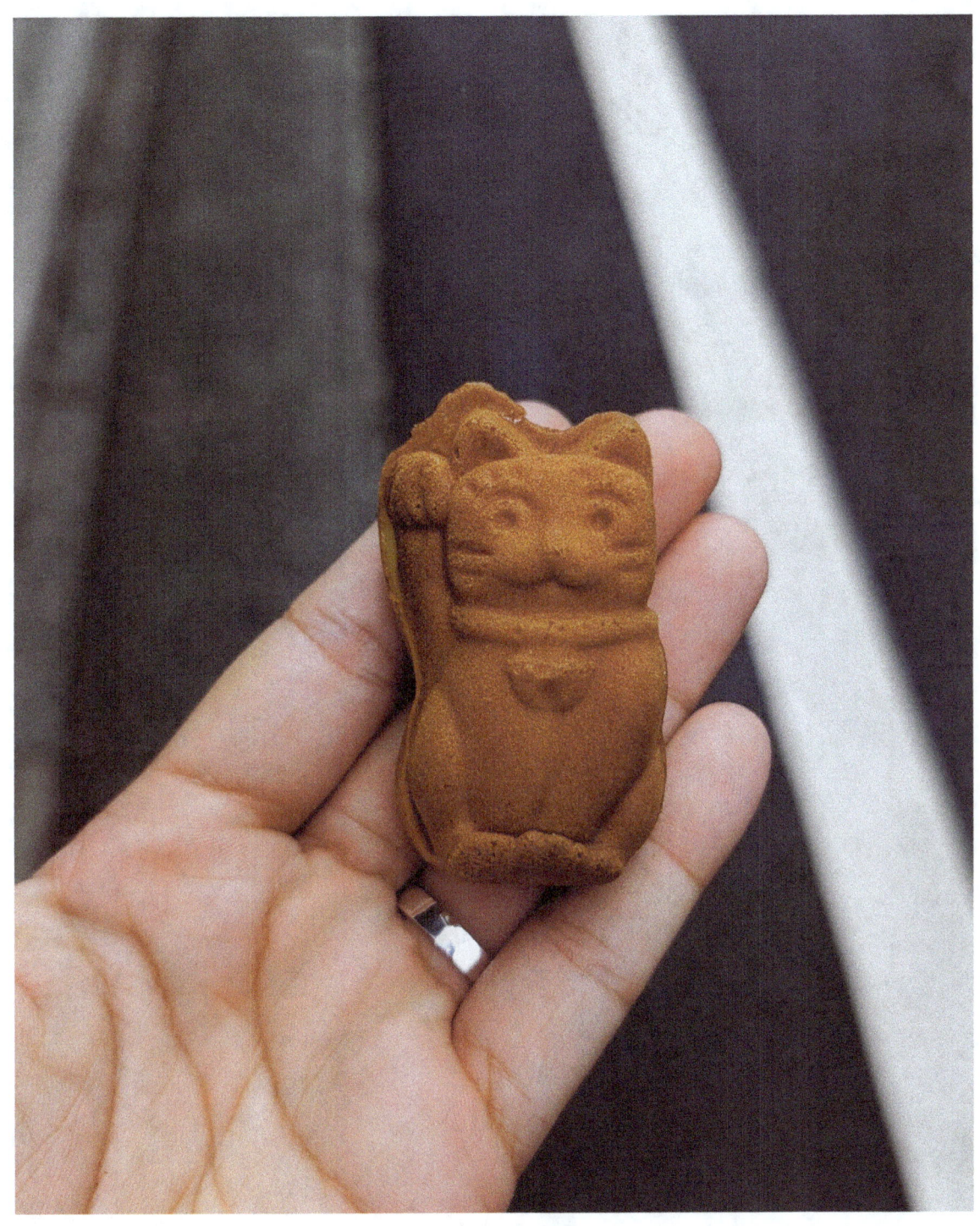

The fortune cookie in the shape of a cat.

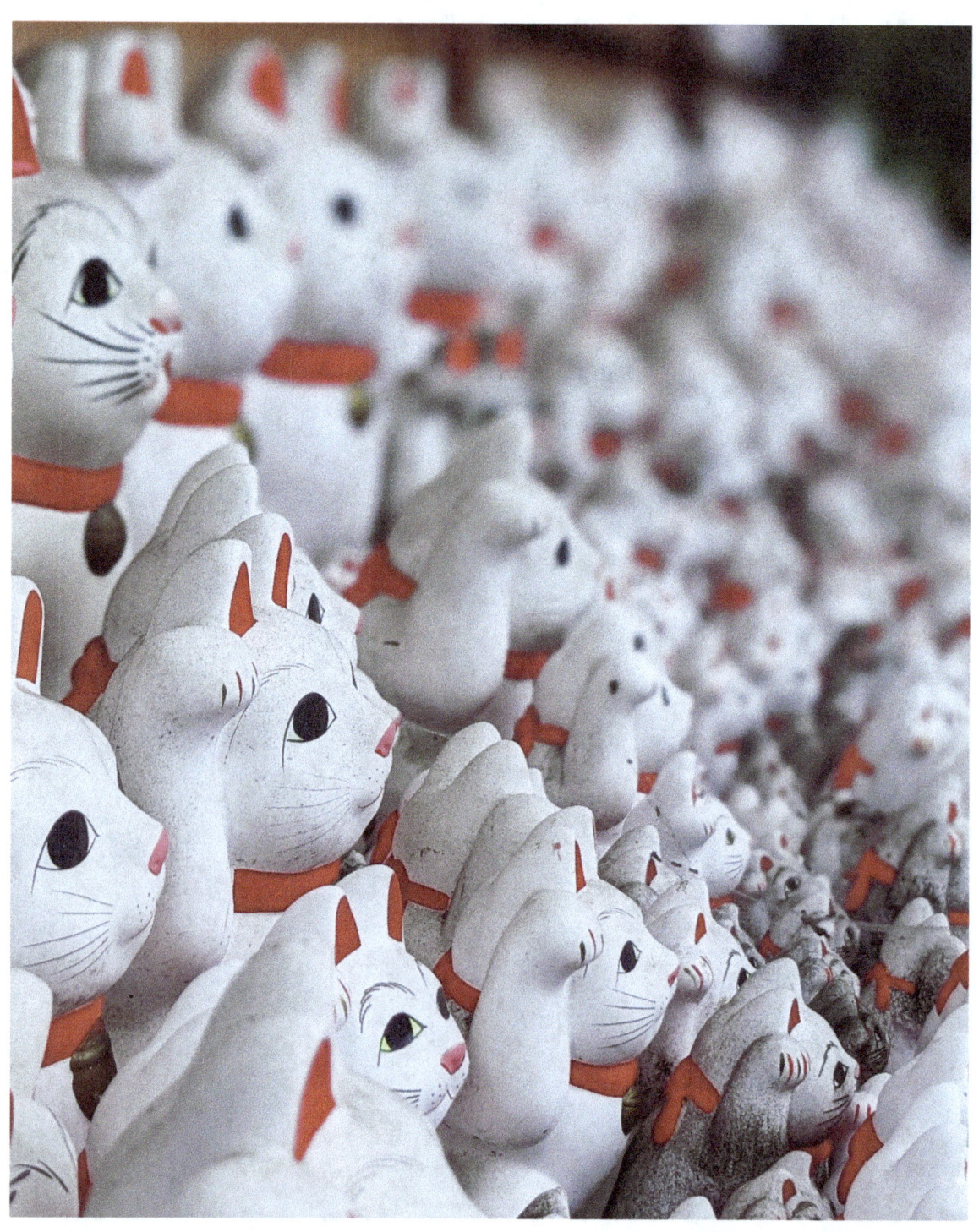

Or thousands of cats.

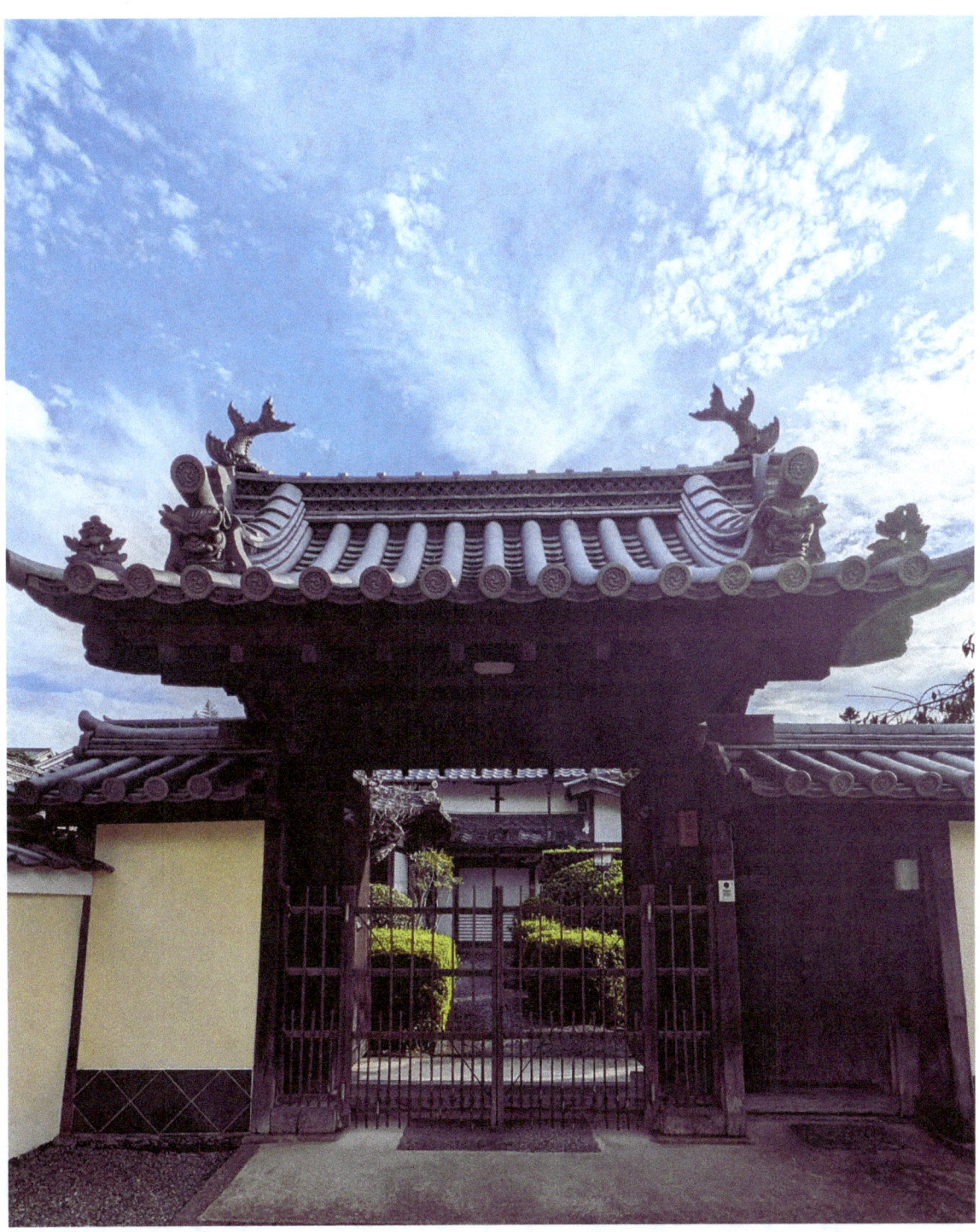

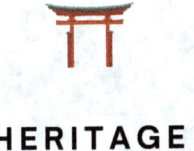

HERITAGE

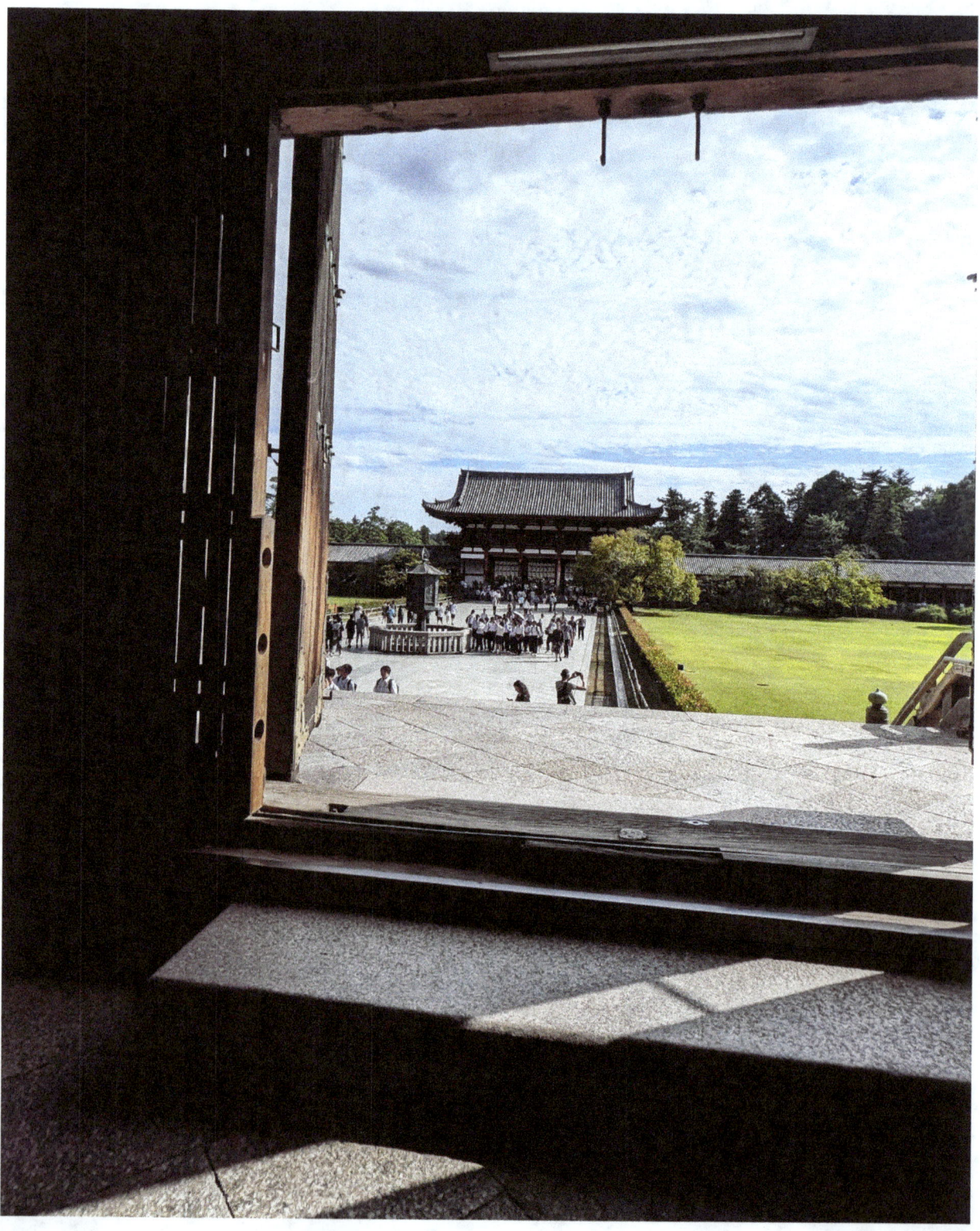

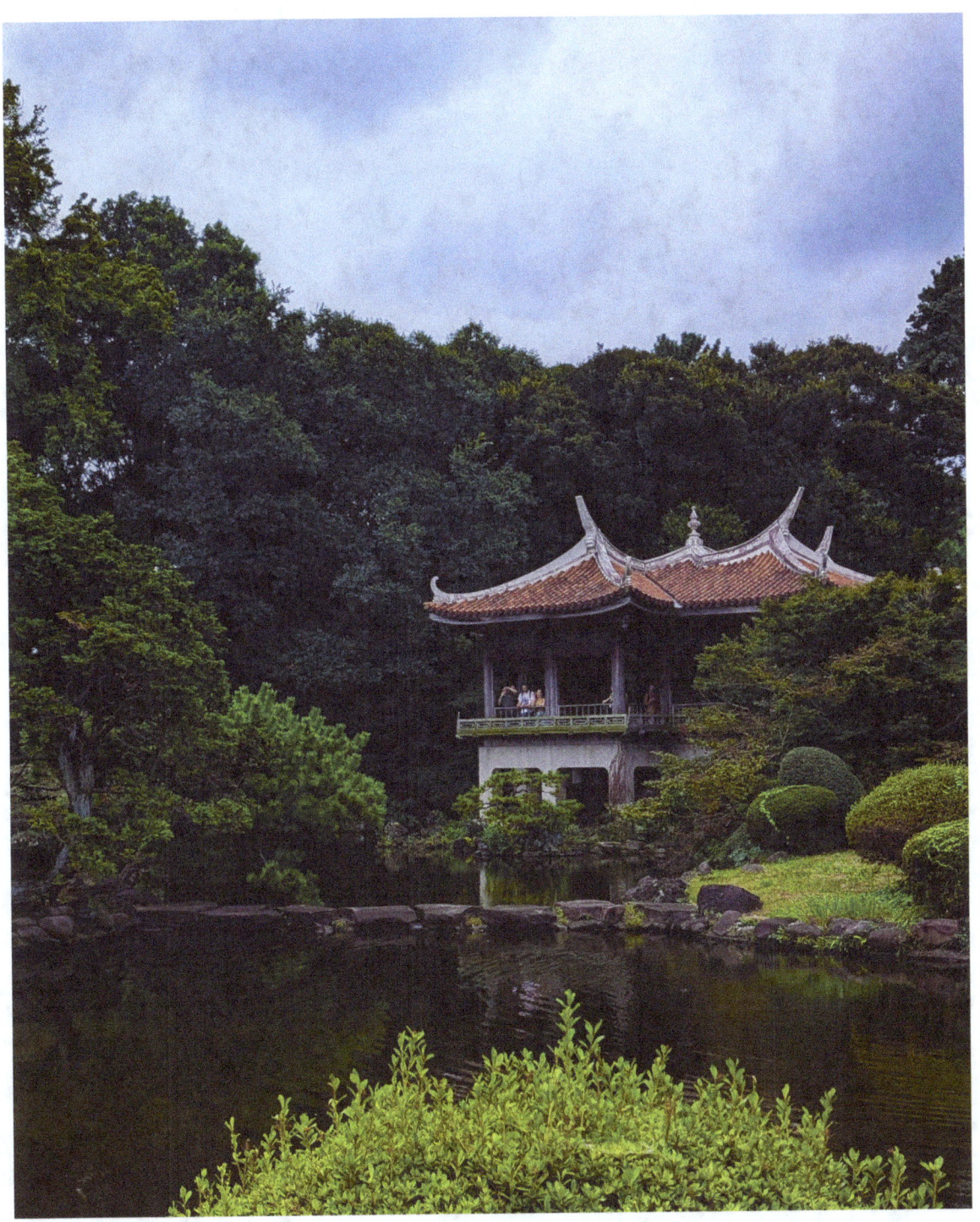

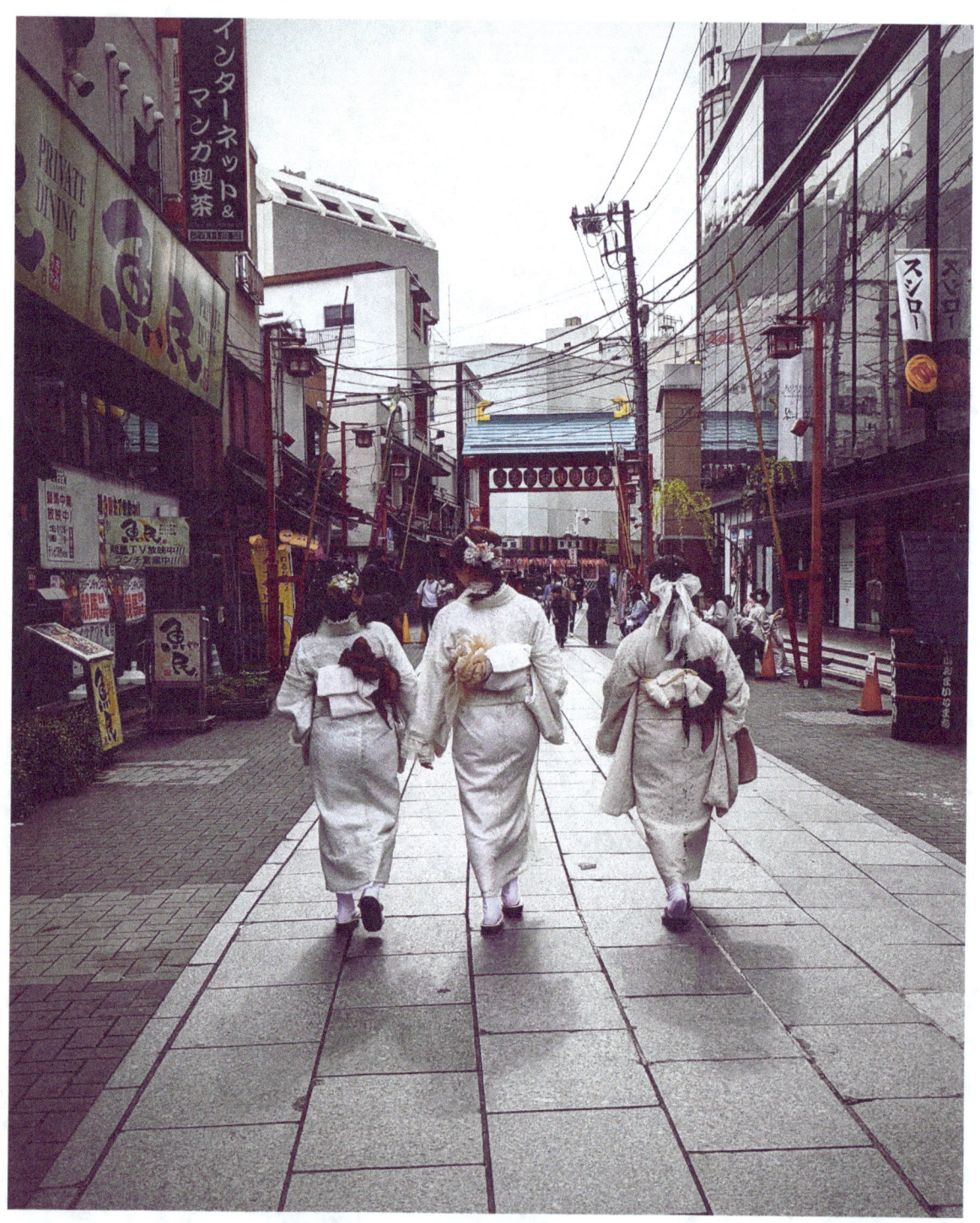

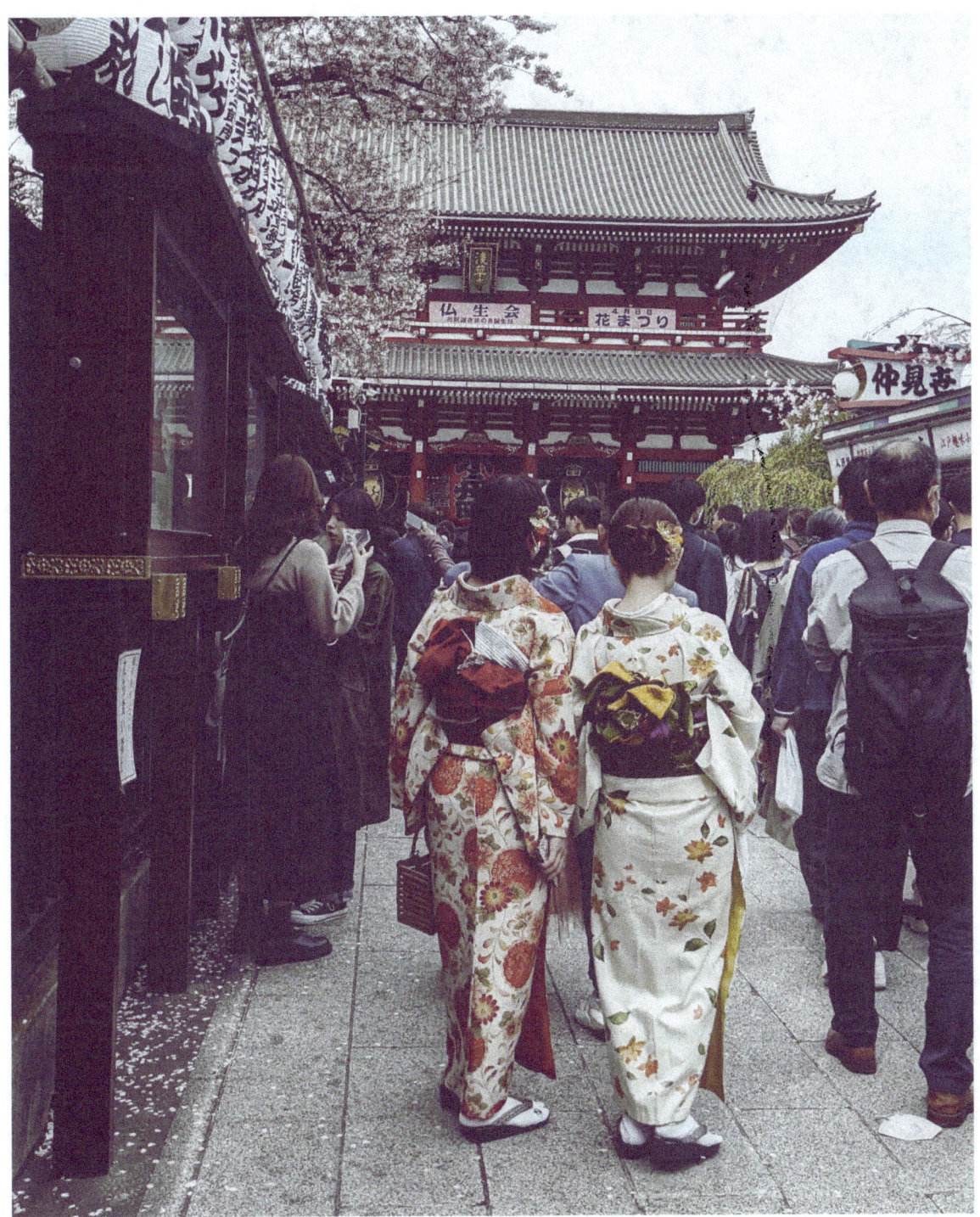

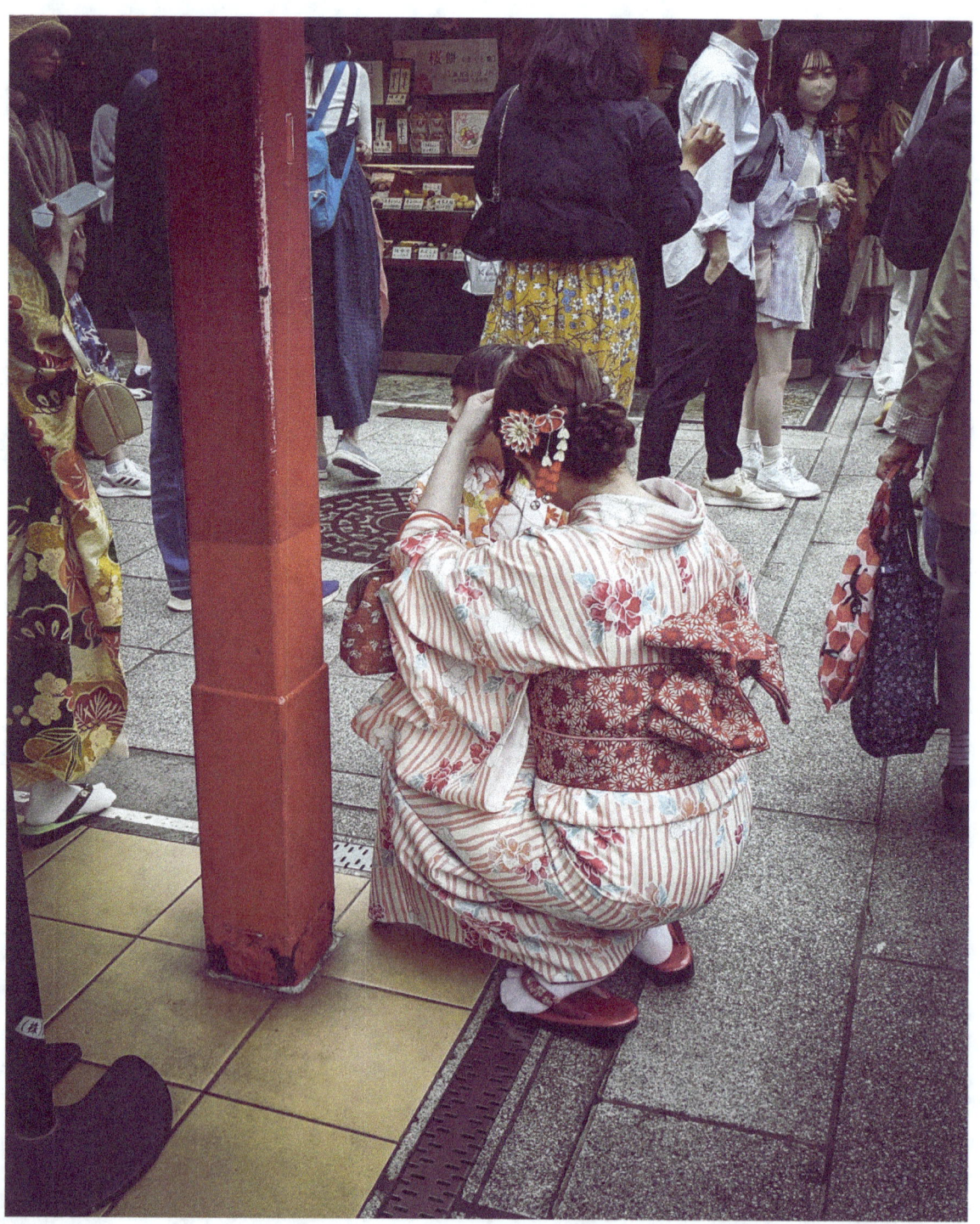

I thought I had dreamed that landscape, but it was real.

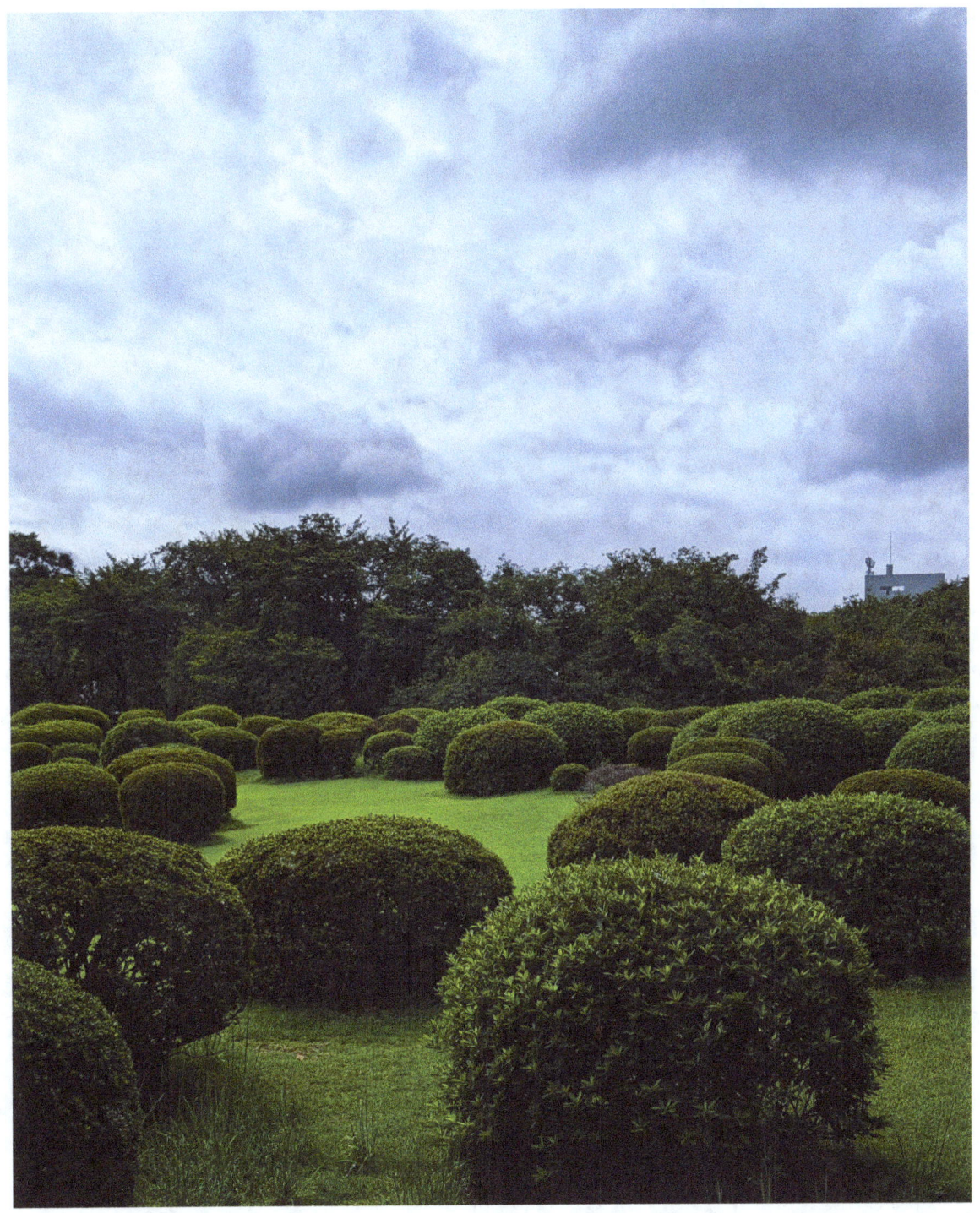

NEVER ENDING BEAUTY

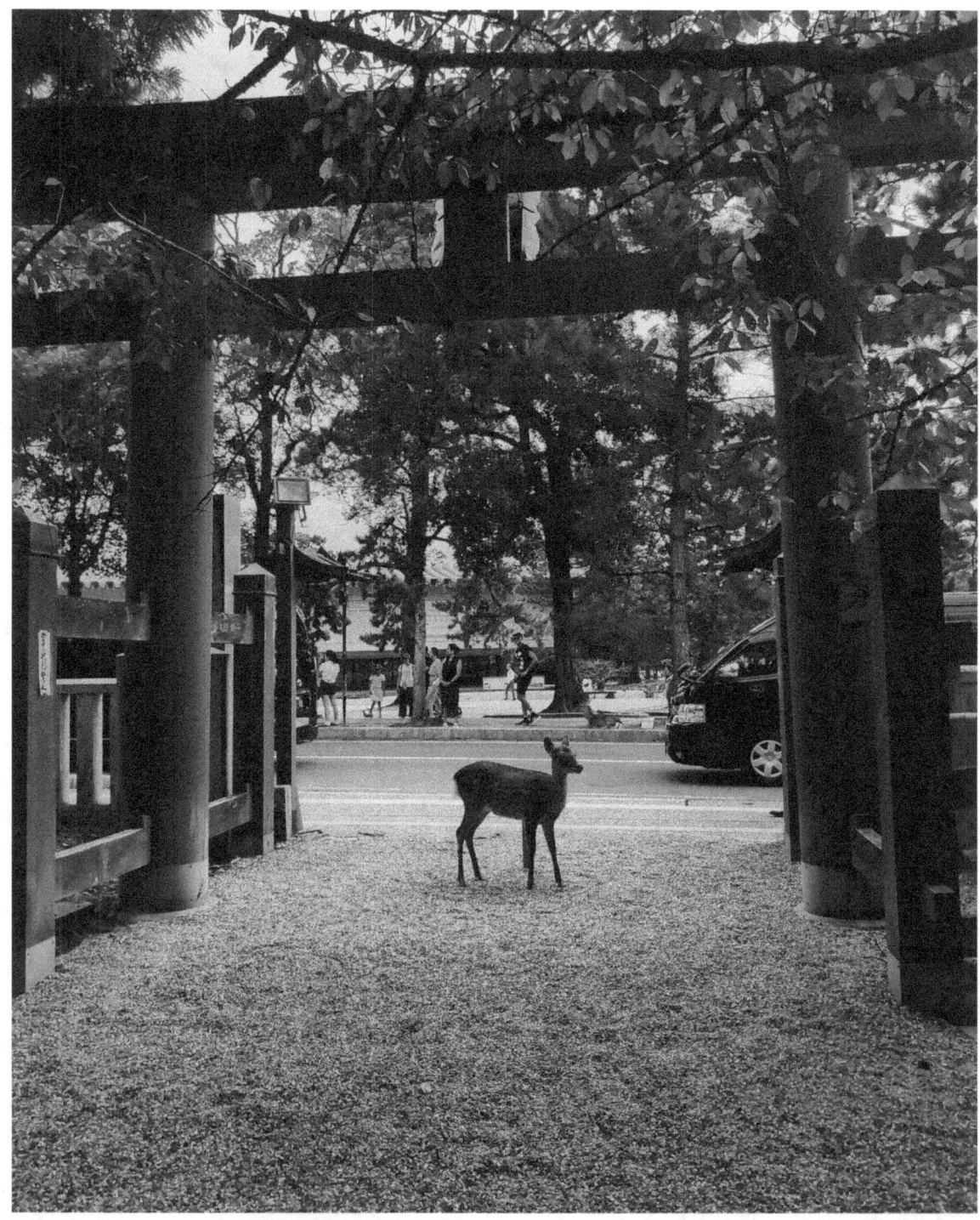

The tori welcomes something sacred, divine and eternal.

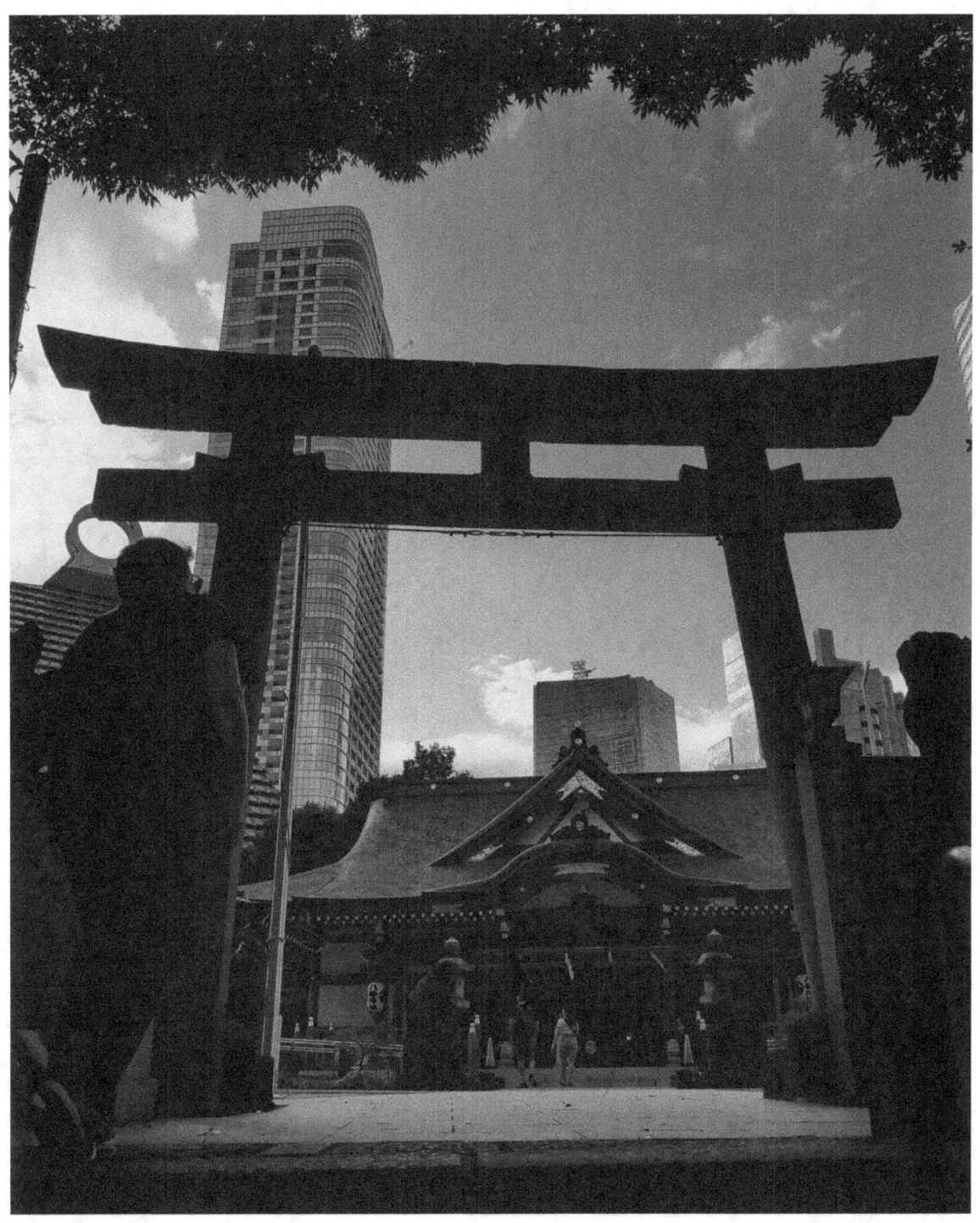

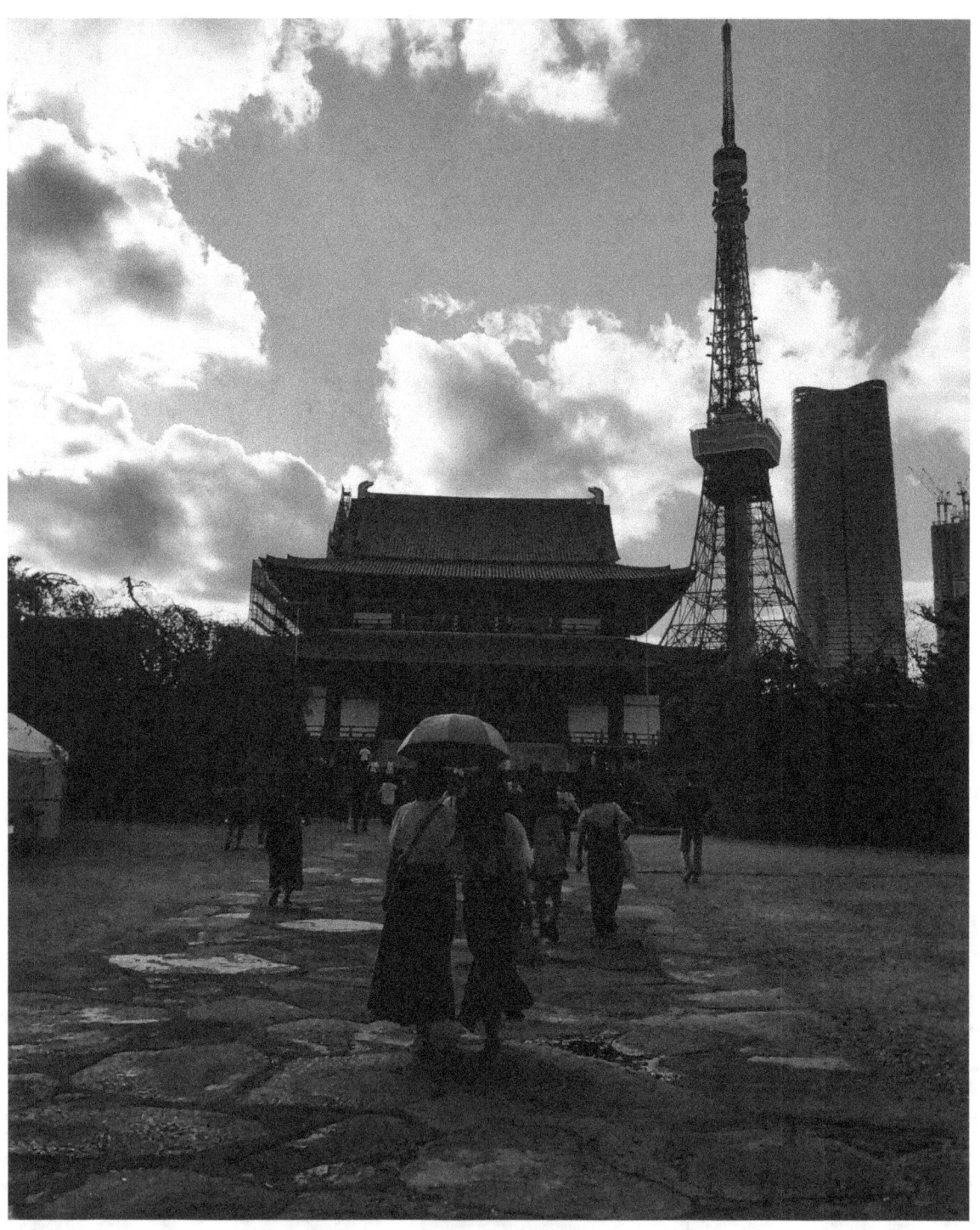

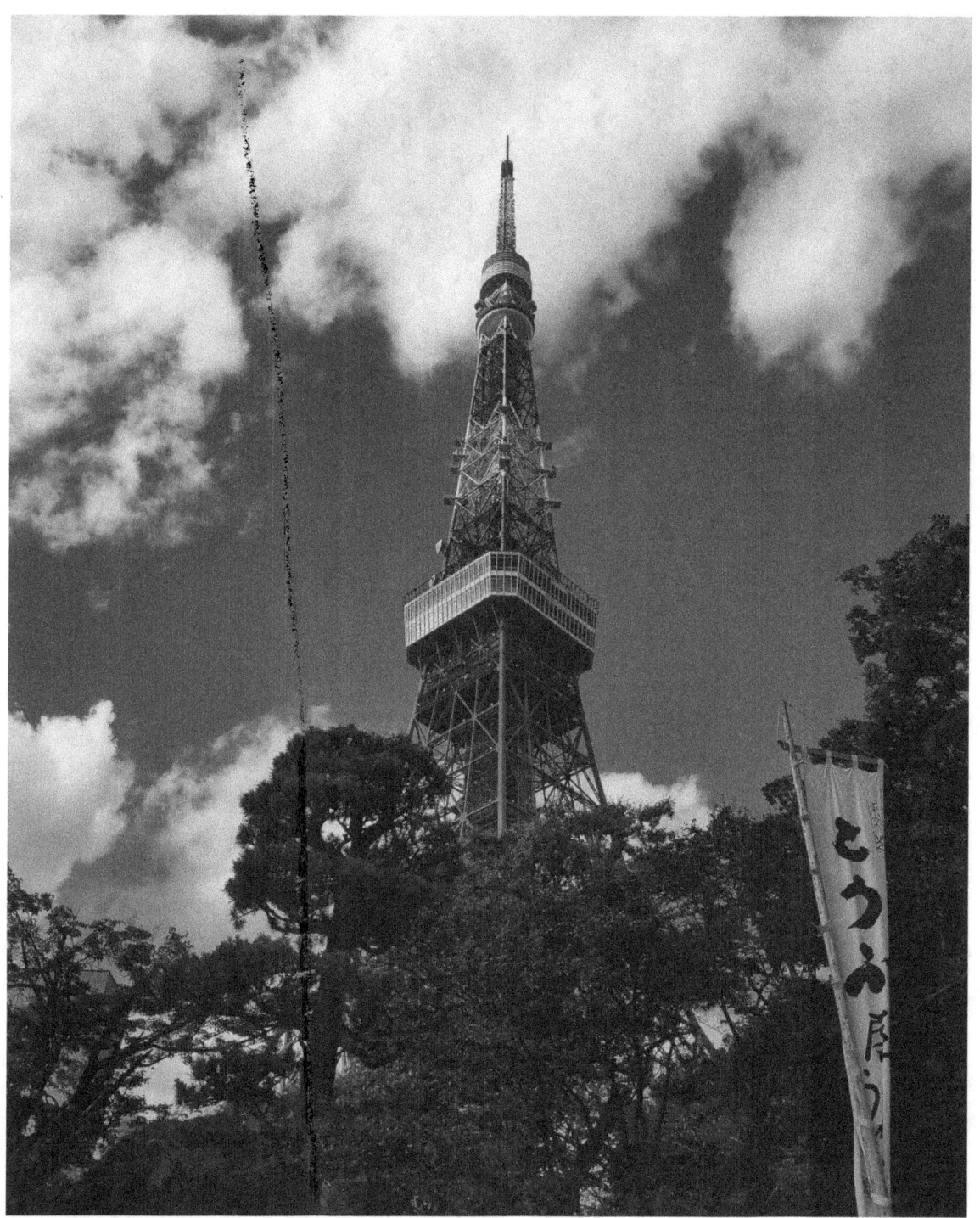

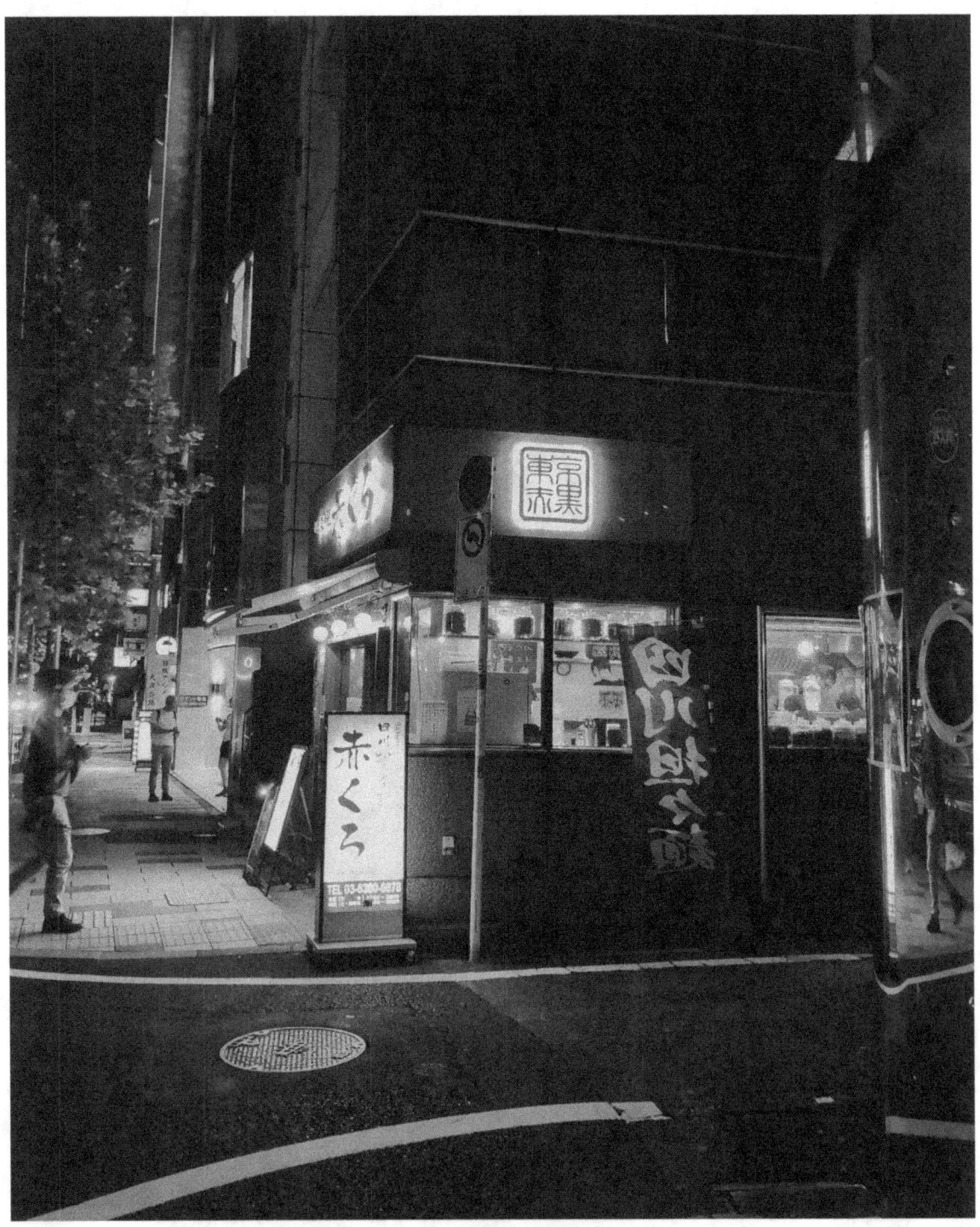

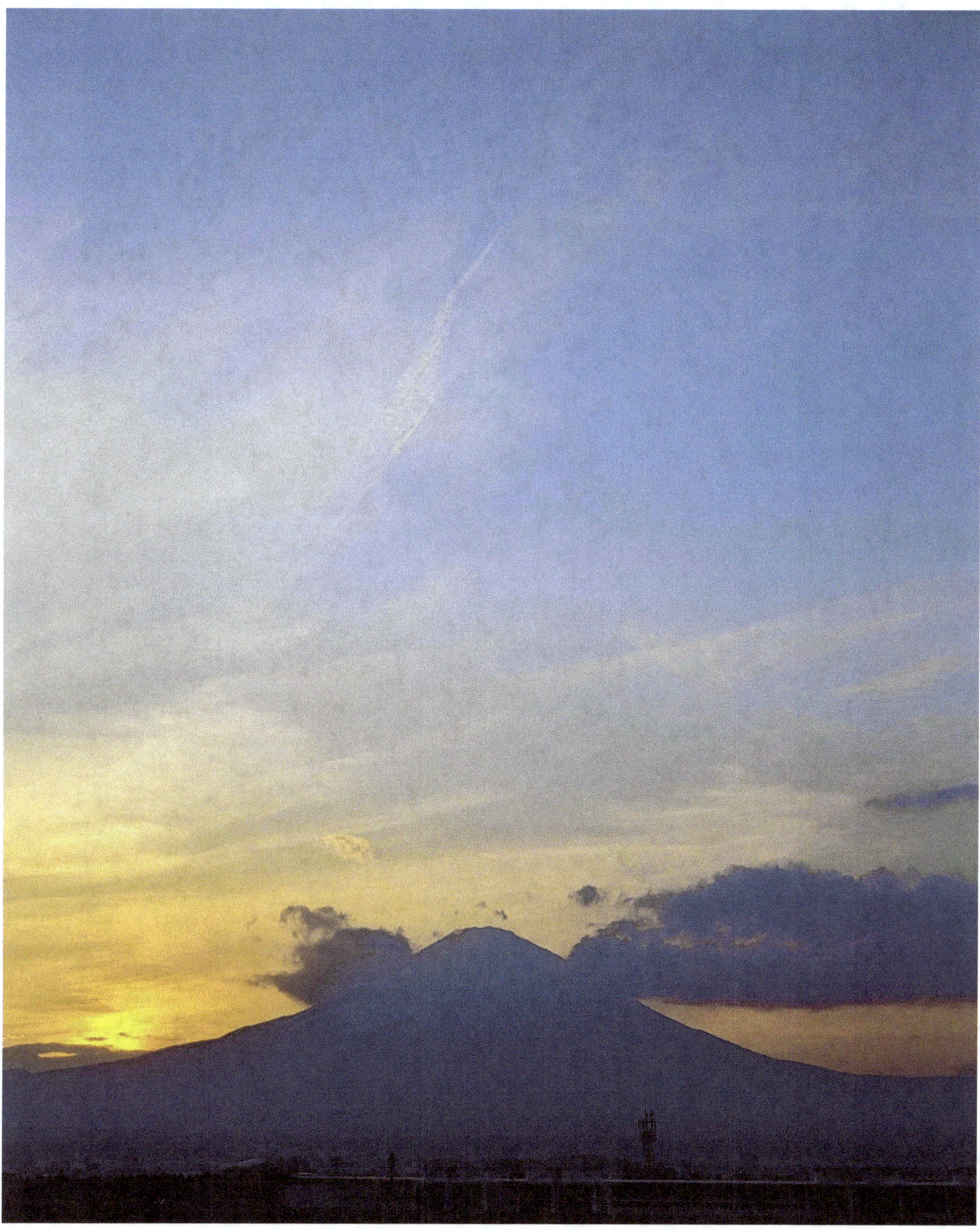

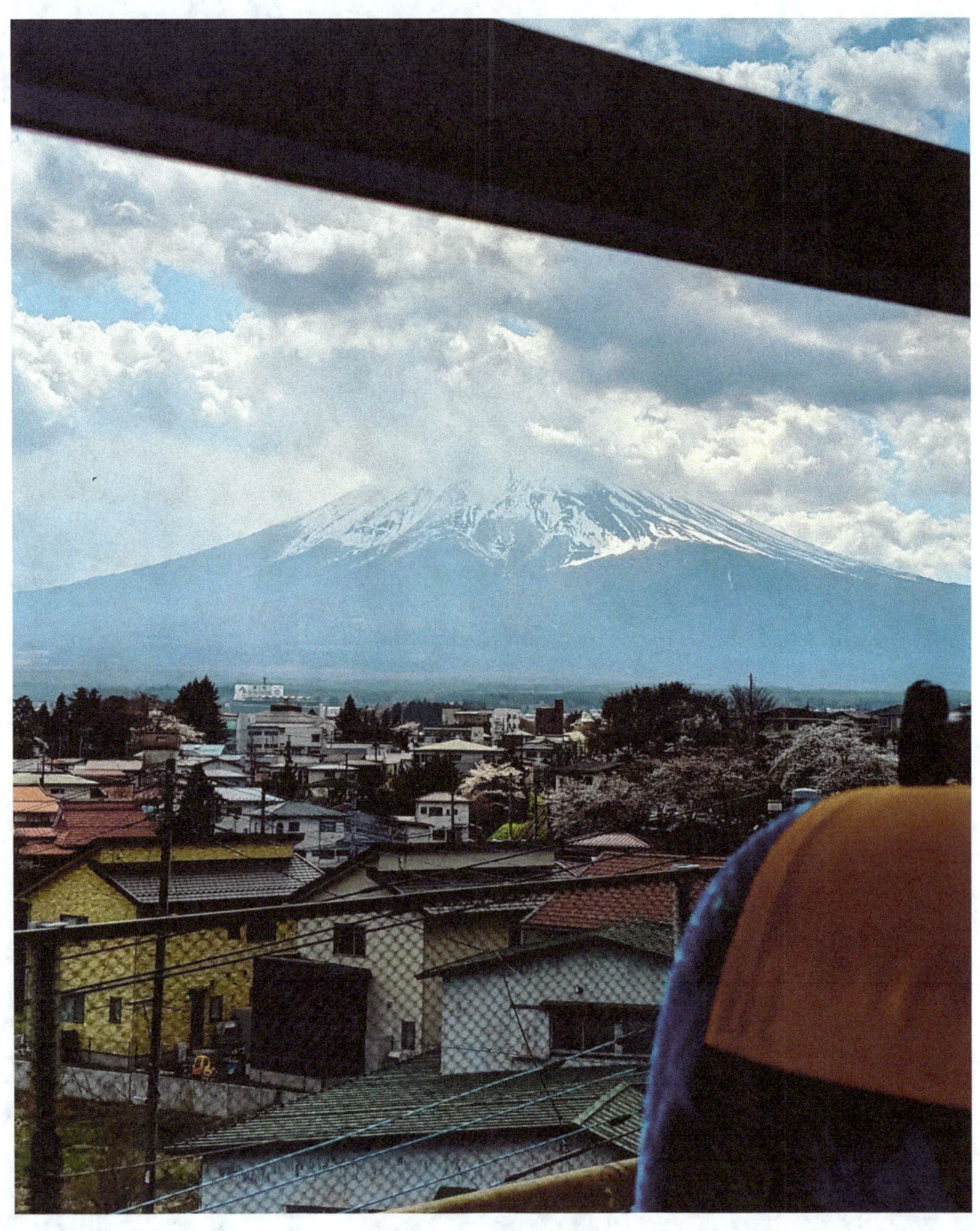

There's something magnetic about Mount Fuji...
you never take your eyes off it.

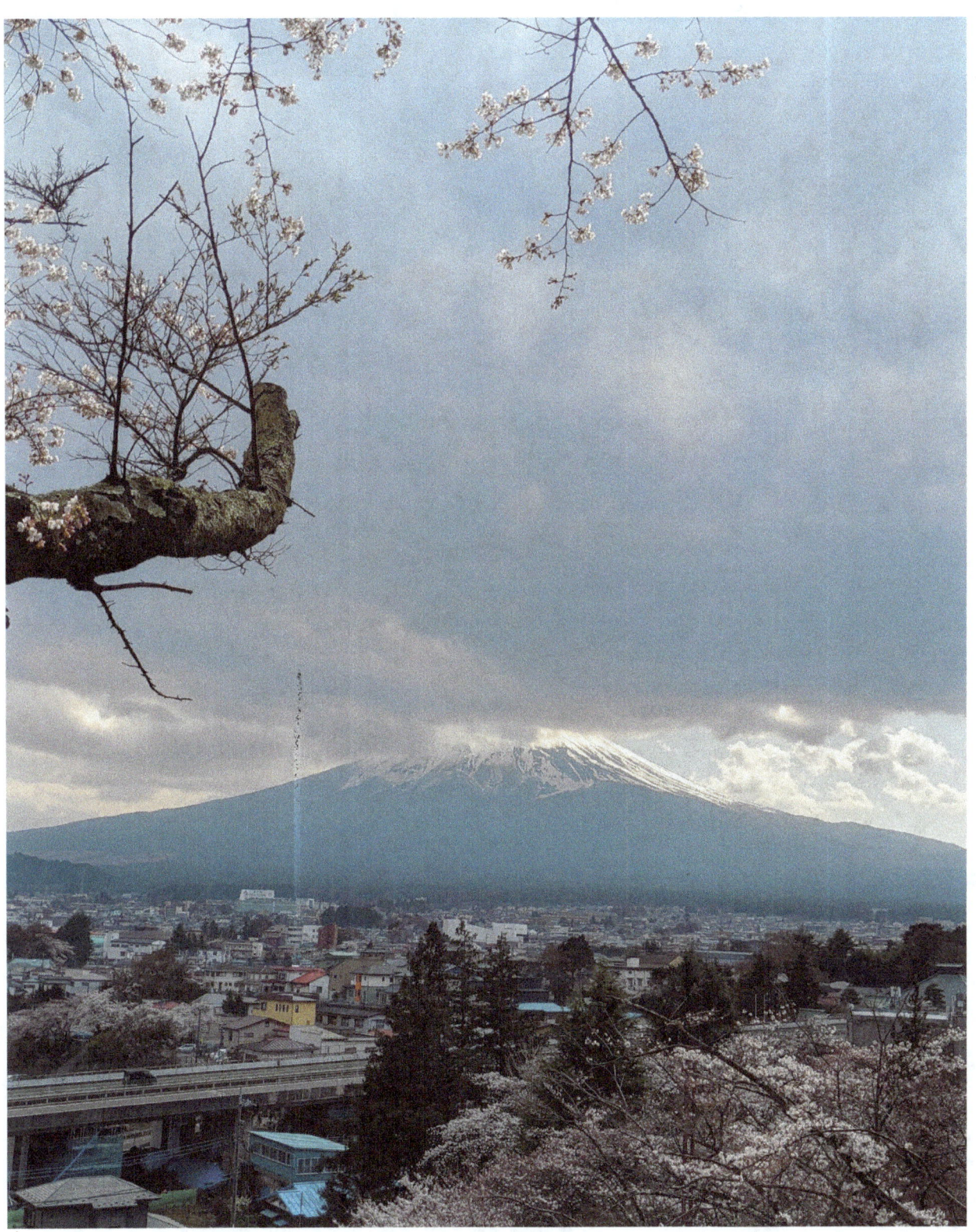

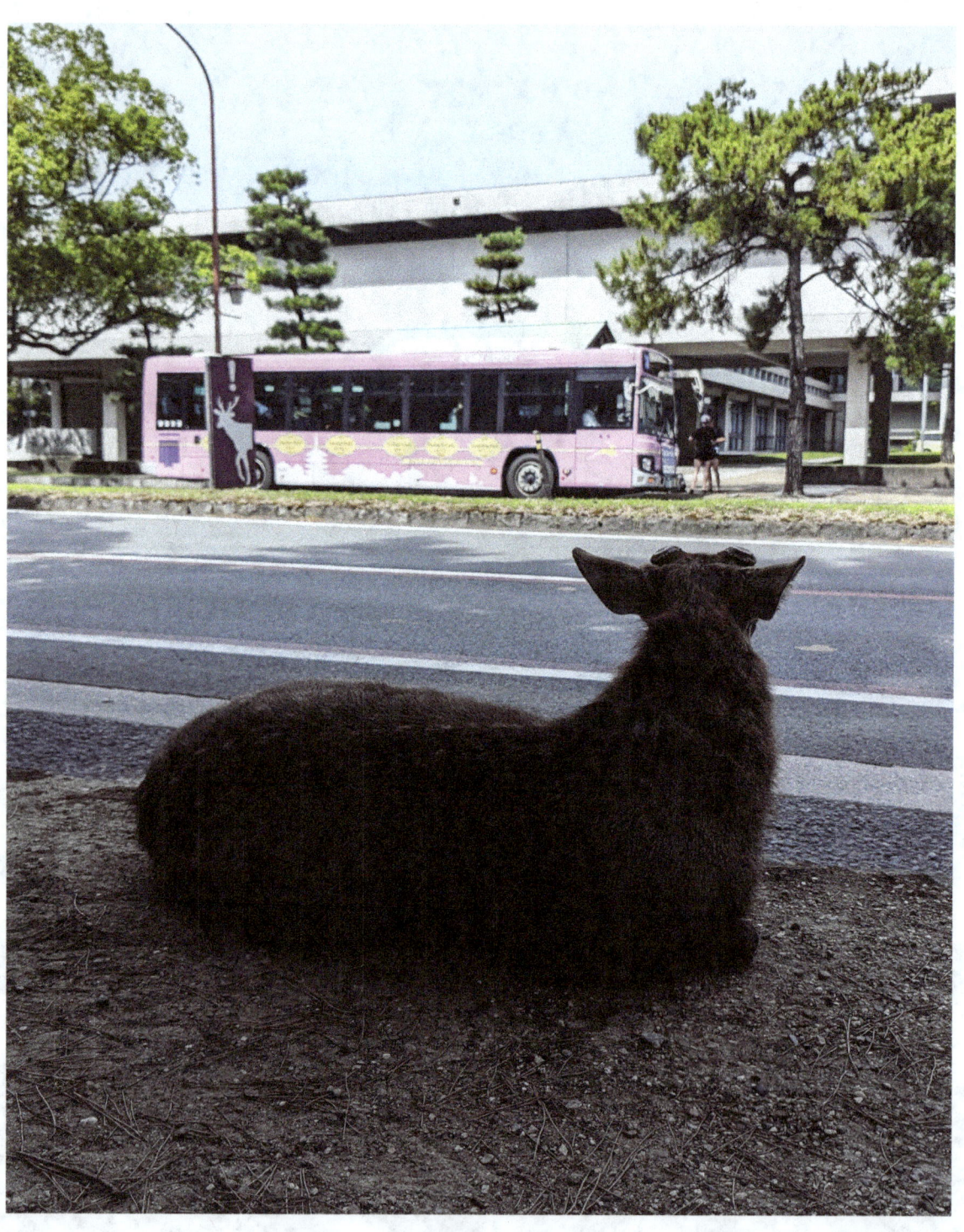

Nara, land of deers.

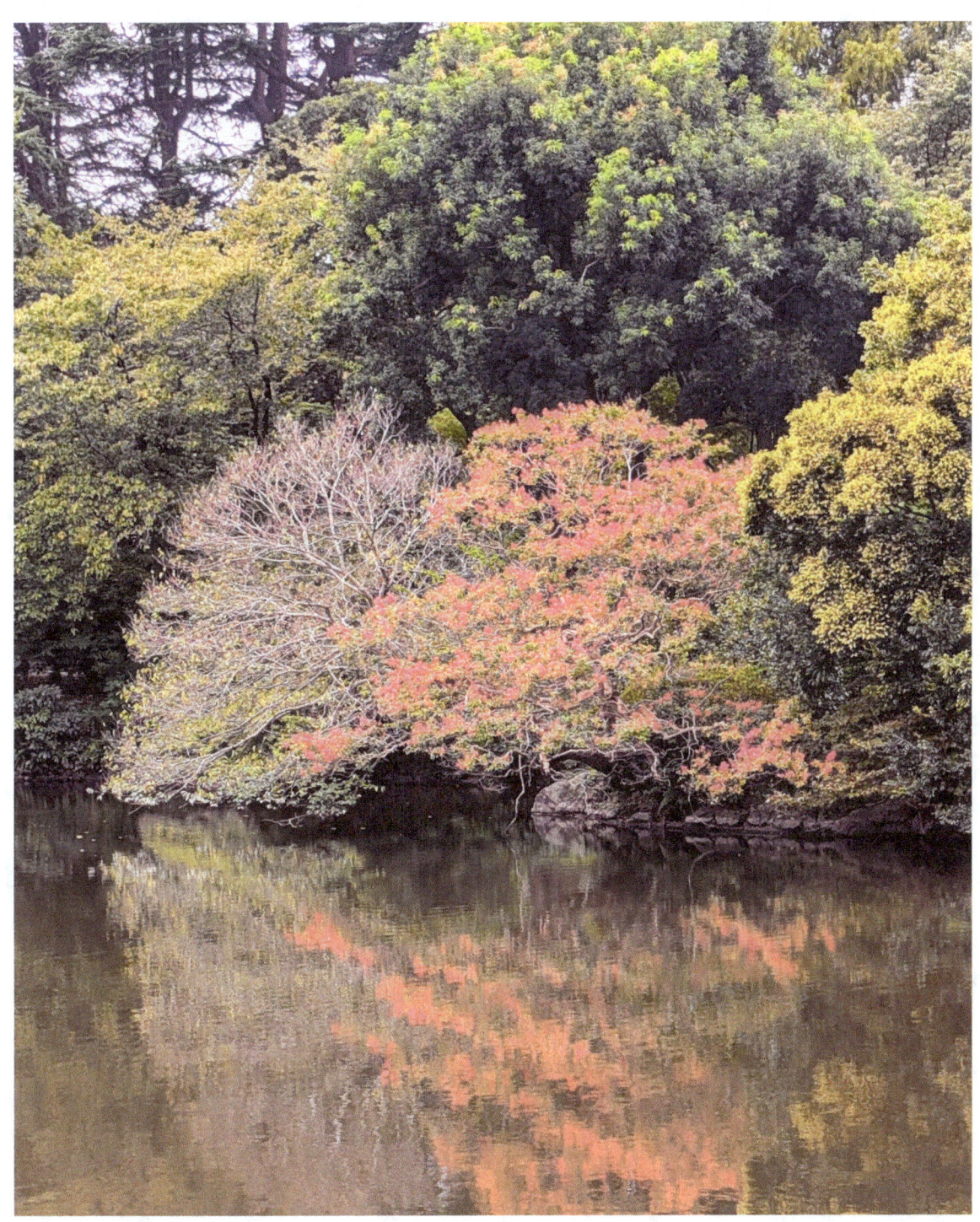

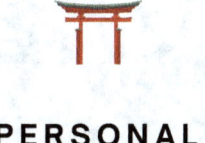

PERSONAL

Reading a manga in a cafe on a rainy day was the perfect plan.

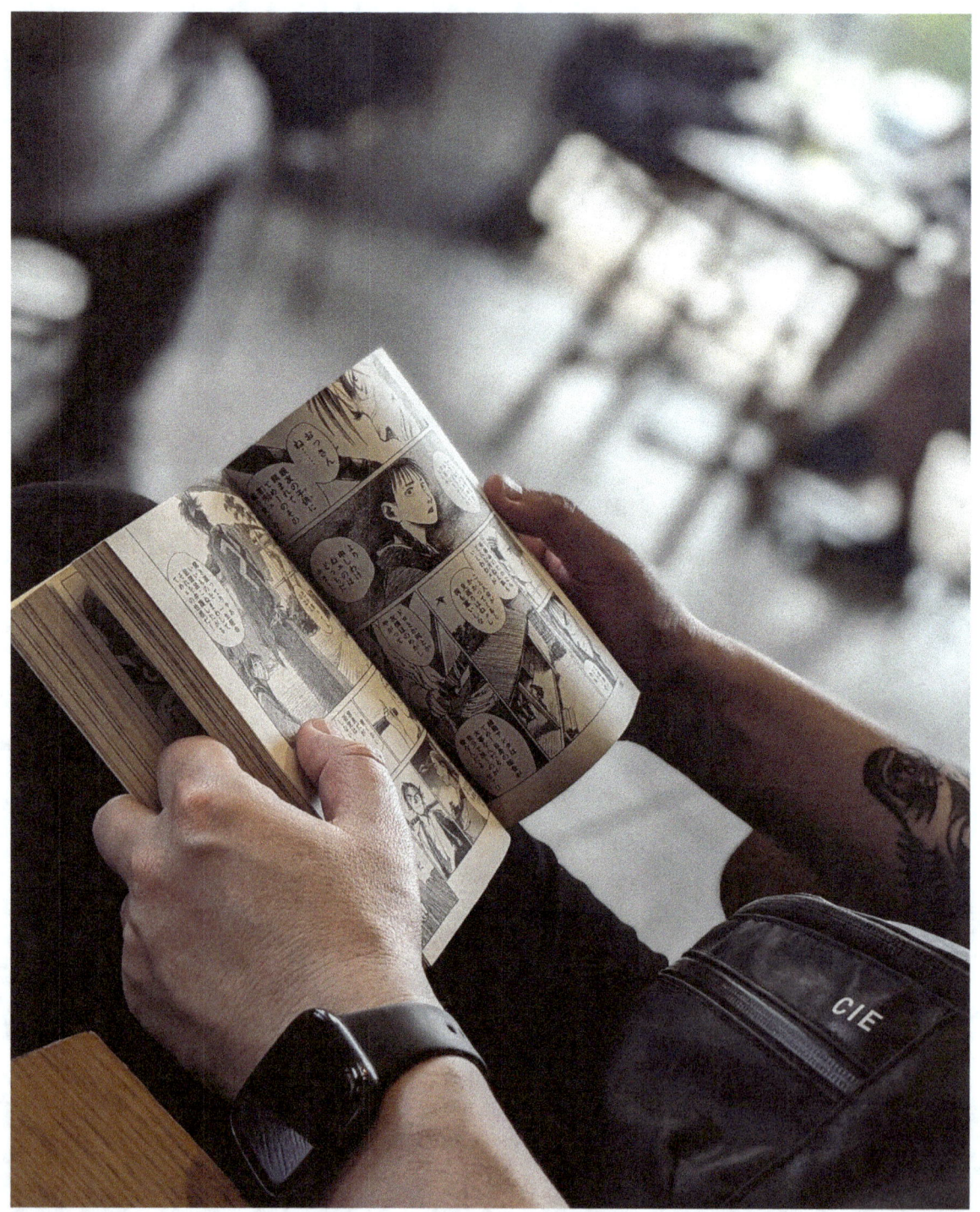

Sakura season on the Meguro River.

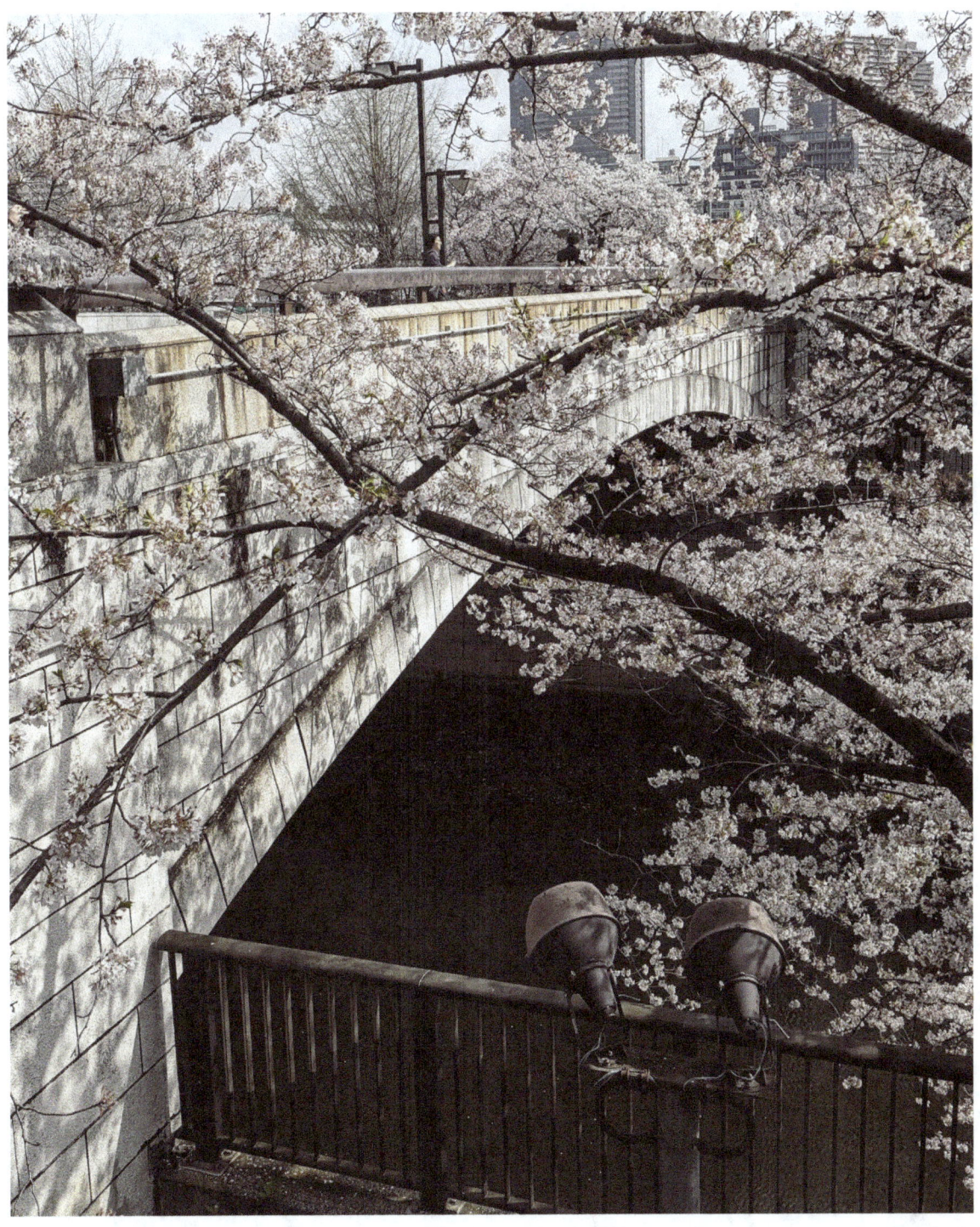

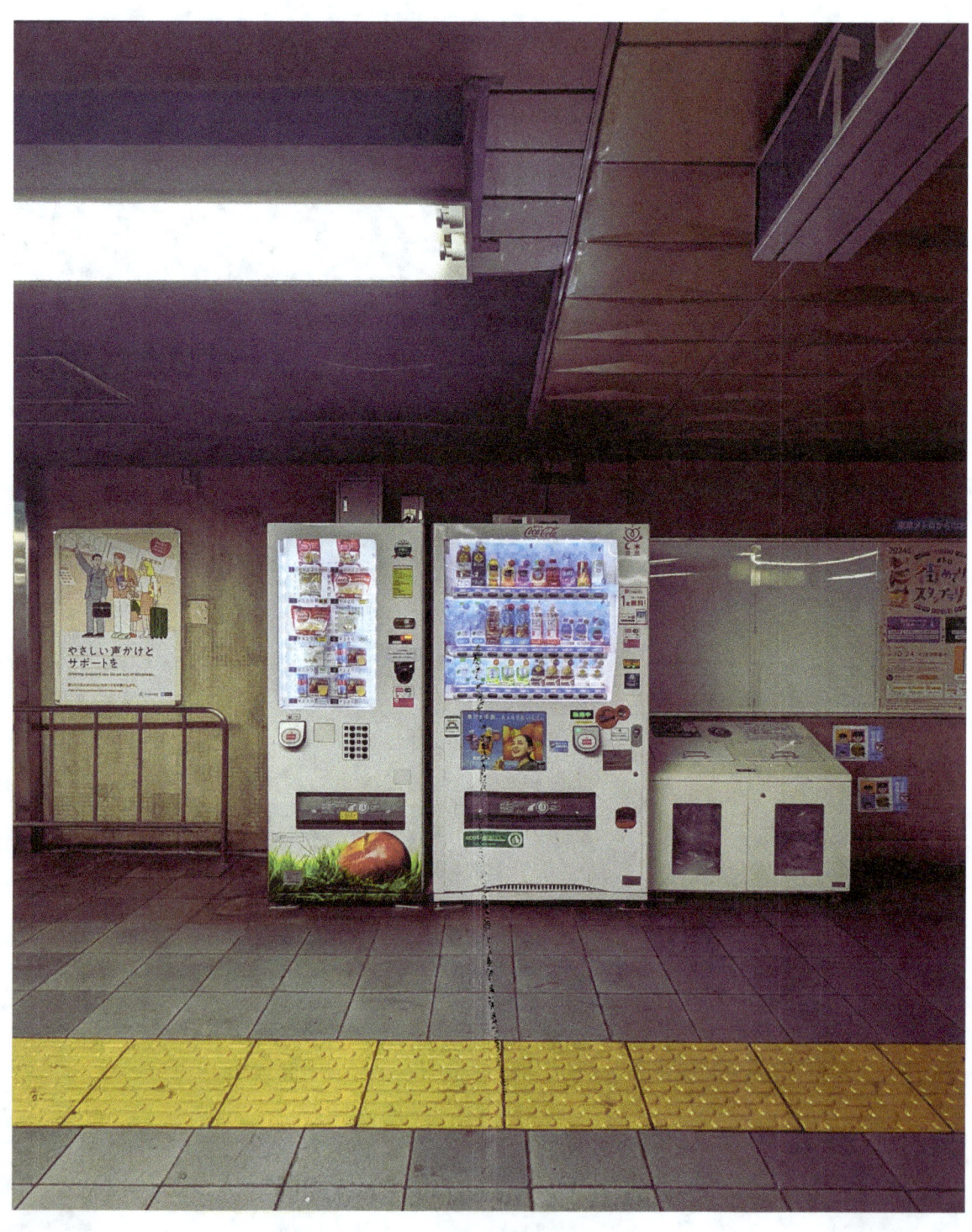

Vending machines are there in every corner, like saviors in hellish summers.

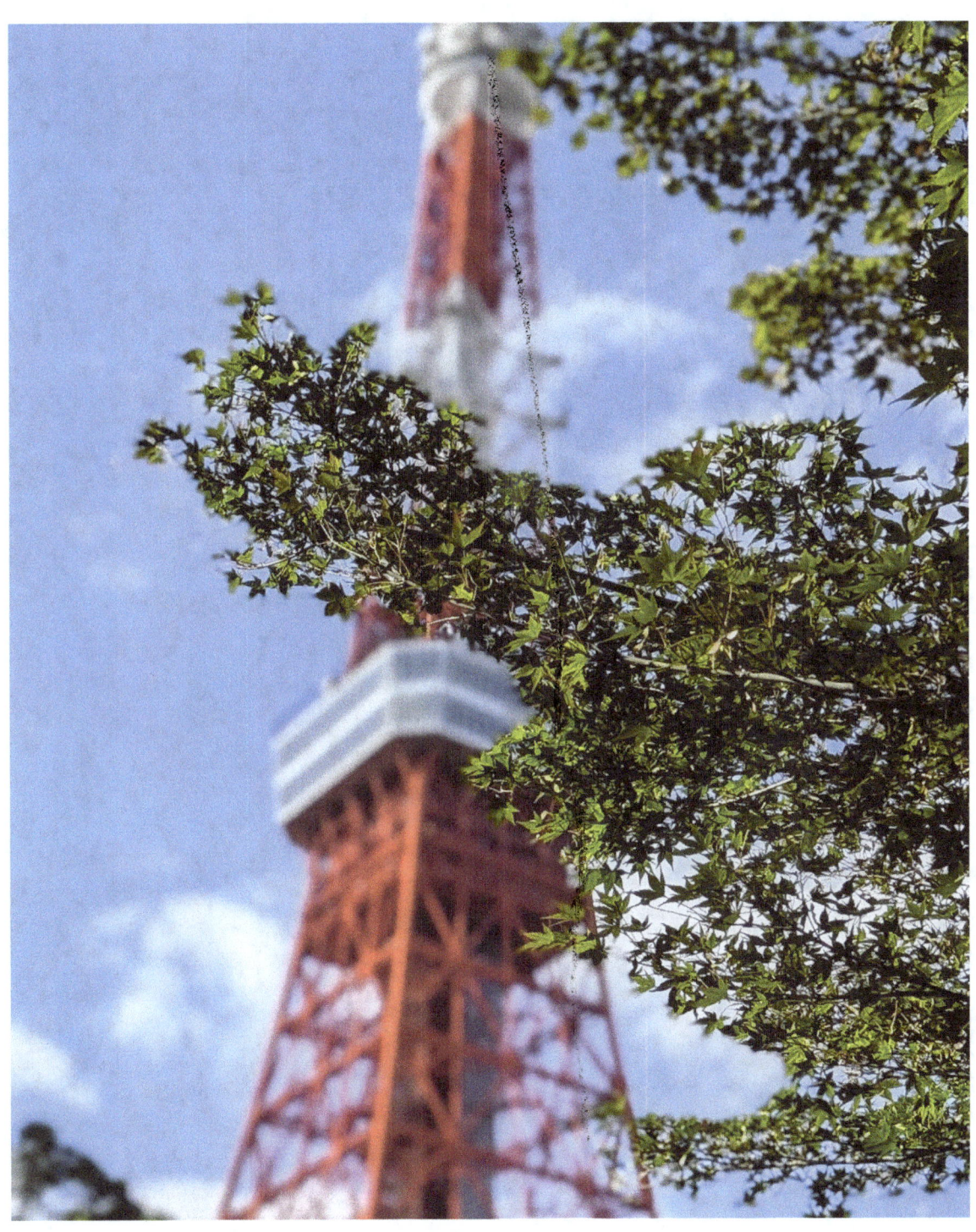

The beautiful green maple.

The transparent umbrellas on which the lights and flashes bounce.

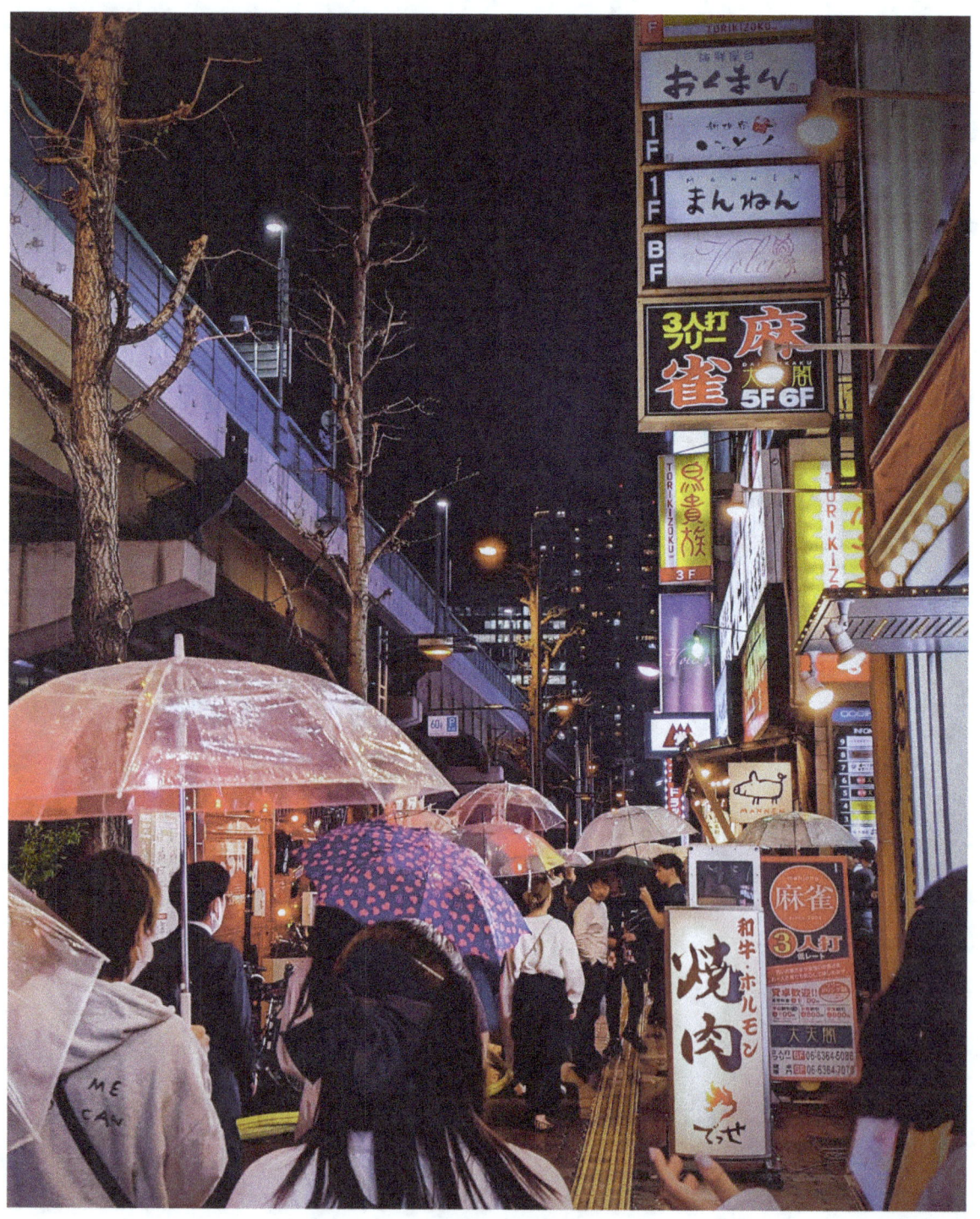

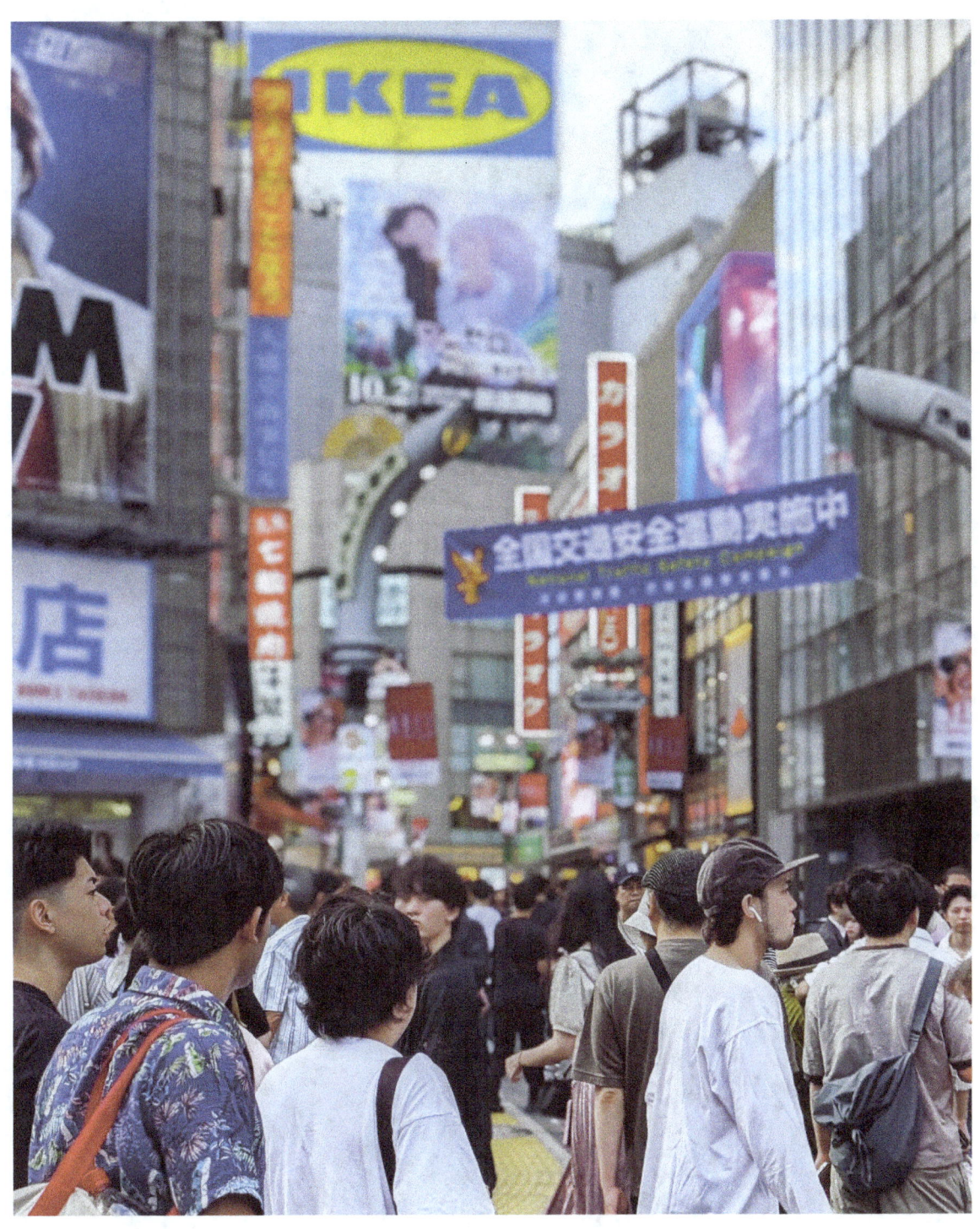

Shibuya Crossing is the perfect place to get lost.

Contemplate the sakura blossom, up close.

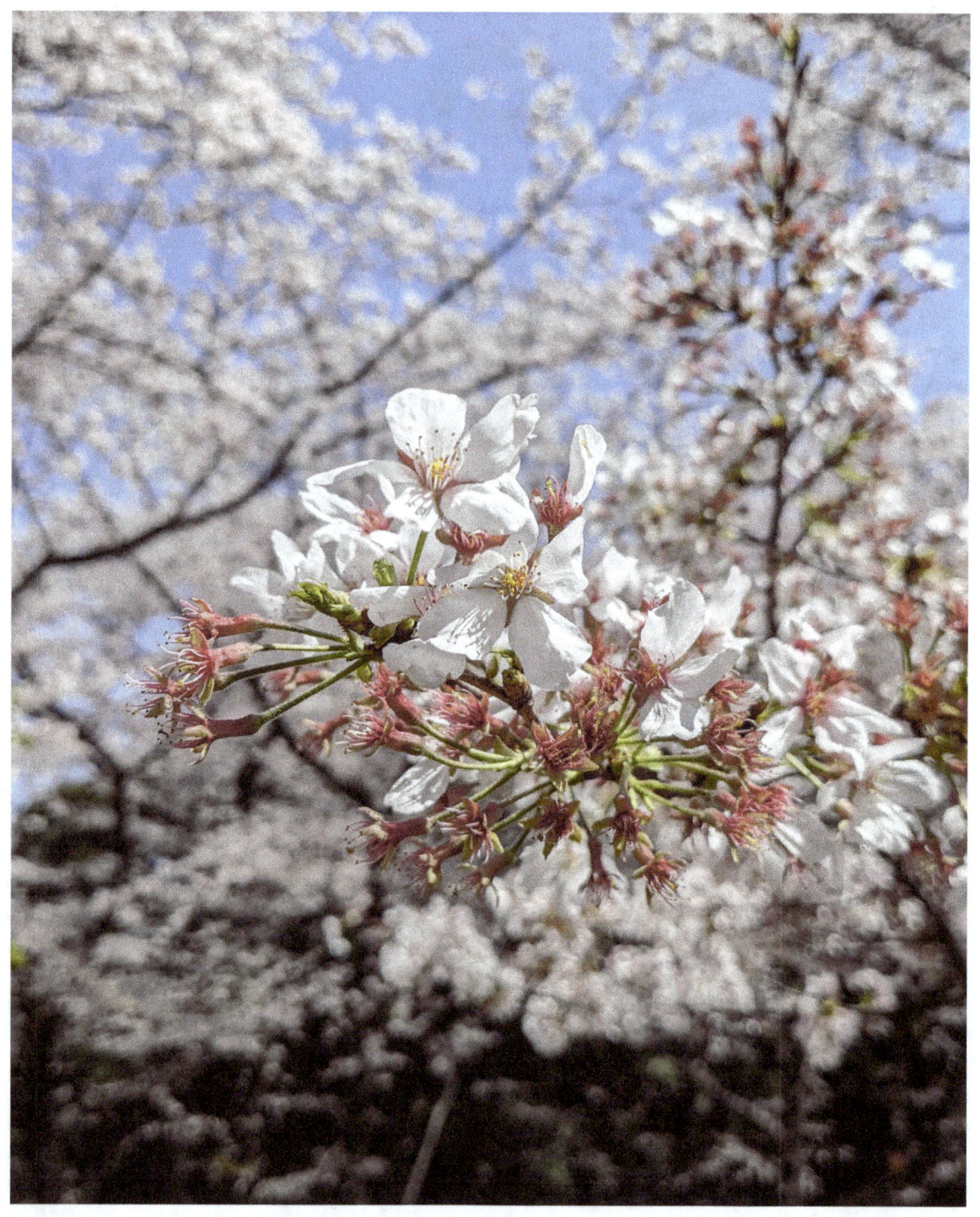

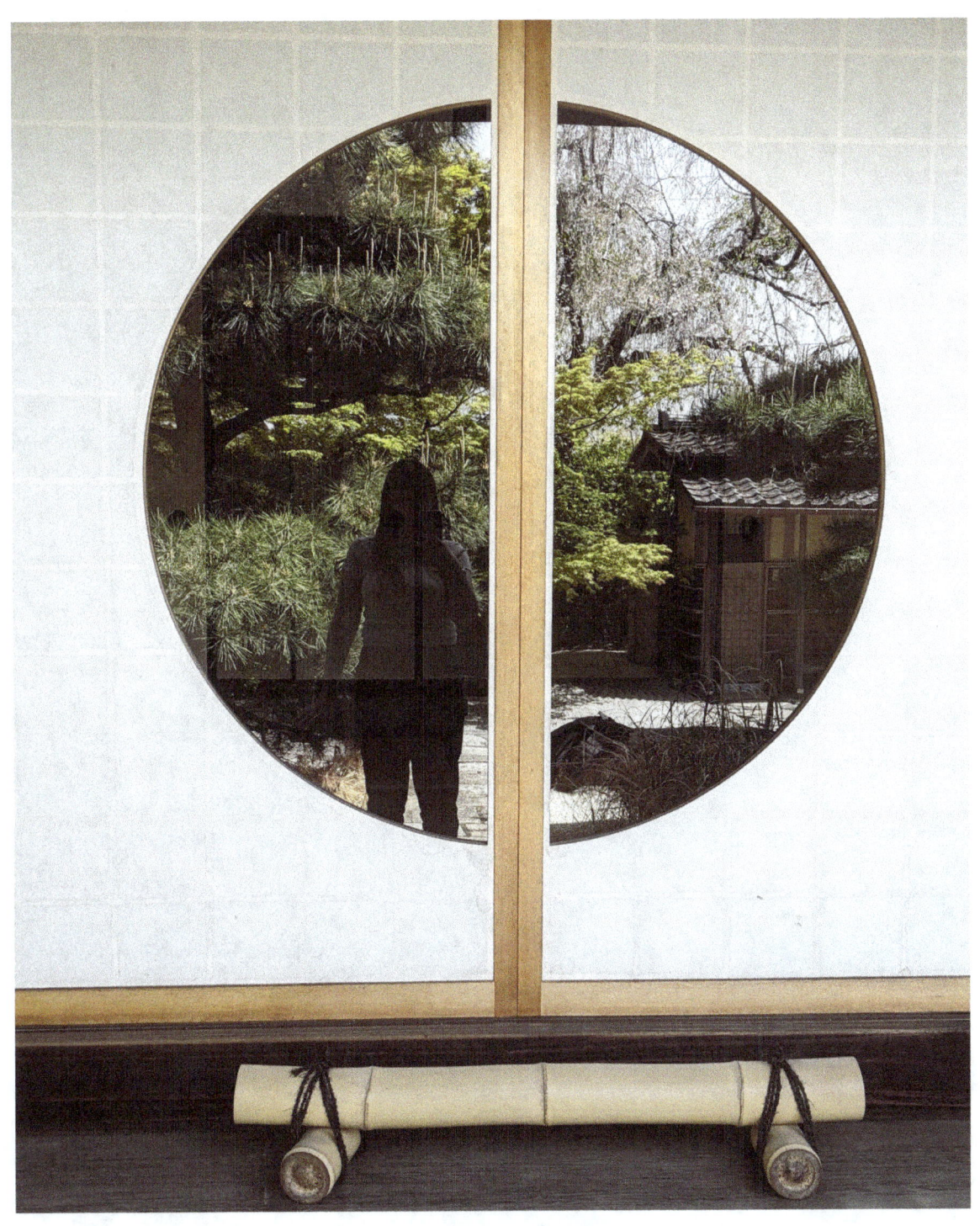

Seeing myself reflected in a temple in Kyoto,
"I'm really here."

www.ingramcontent.com/pod-product-compliance
Lightning Source LLC
Chambersburg PA
CBHW062335220526
45469CB00008B/2718